'06

D0915948

Careers in Focus

REAL ESTATE

Ferguson

An imprint of Infobase Publishing

Careers in Focus: Real Estate

Copyright © 2006 by Infobase Publishing

Ferguson
An imprint of Infobase Publishing
132 West 31st Street
New York NY 10001

Library of Congress Cataloging-in-Publication Data

Careers in focus. Real estate.
    p. cm.
  Includes index.
  ISBN 0-8160-6566-7 (hc: alk. paper)
  1. Real estate business—Vocational guidance—Juvenile literature. I. J. G.
Ferguson Publishing Company. II. Title: Real estate.
  HD1375.C3545 2007
  333.33023—dc22   2006009221

Ferguson books are available at special discounts when purchased in bulk quantities for businesses, associations, institutions, or sales promotions. Please call our Special Sales Department in New York at (212) 967-8800 or (800) 322-8755.

You can find Ferguson on the World Wide Web at http://www.fergpubco.com

Text design by David Strelecky

Printed in the United States of America

MP Hermitage 10 9 8 7 6 5 4 3 2 1

This book is printed on acid-free paper.

Table of Contents

Introduction

Careers in Focus: Real Estate describes a variety of careers in the demanding, yet rewarding, world of real estate—in real estate agencies, law firms and courtrooms, government agencies, schools, offices, insurance agencies, and financial institutions, as well as at construction sites and other settings. These careers are as diverse in nature as they are in their earnings and educational requirements. There are opportunities available for those with business and sales acumen (loan officers, real estate agents and brokers, and real estate developers), creativity (architects, writers, and advertising workers), and technical ability (inspectors, surveying and mapping technicians, and surveyors).

Earnings range from less than $14,000 for entry-level clerks to more than $100,000 for experienced real estate lawyers, advertising workers, developers, and other professionals in this highly lucrative industry.

A few of these careers—such as clerks and title searchers—require little formal education, but are excellent starting points for a career in the industry. Others—such as assessors, appraisers, property insurance agents and brokers, and surveyors—require some post-secondary training. The majority of the highest-paying careers (such as architects, financial institution officers, risk managers, and real estate writers) in the real estate industry require a bachelor's degree or higher. The career of real estate lawyer requires a law degree.

The real estate industry is subject to fluctuations of the economy. Low interest rates encourage people to seek mortgages and buy property, which stimulates the real estate industry. The real estate market can be strong in some parts of the country and weak in other parts of the country. Often an area will be strong for a certain amount of time, followed by a decrease in the number of real estate transactions.

Technology is improving the productivity of agents and brokers. Real estate companies and sellers are making more information available on the Internet and agents are able to serve a much larger number of customers. The use of advanced technology is likely to discourage part-time and temporary real estate work because of the investment costs and the competition with full-time workers.

Each article in this book discusses a particular real estate occupation in detail. The articles in *Careers in Focus: Real Estate* appear in Ferguson's *Encyclopedia of Careers and Vocational Guidance,*

I

but have been updated and revised with the latest information from the U.S. Department of Labor, professional organizations, and other sources. The following paragraphs detail the sections and features that appear in the book.

The **Quick Facts** section provides a brief summary of the career, including recommended school subjects, personal skills, work environment, minimum educational requirements, salary ranges, certification or licensing requirements, and employment outlook. This section also provides acronyms and identification numbers for the following government classification indexes: the *Dictionary of Occupational Titles* (DOT), the *Guide for Occupational Exploration* (GOE), the National Occupational Classification (NOC) index, and the Occupational Information Network (O*NET)-Standard Occupational Classification System (SOC) index. The DOT, GOE, and O*NET-SOC indexes have been created by the U.S. government; the NOC index is Canada's career classification system. Readers can use the identification numbers listed in the Quick Facts section of each article to access further information about a career. Print editions of the DOT (*Dictionary of Occupational Titles*. Indianapolis, Ind.: JIST Works, 1991) and GOE (*Guide for Occupational Exploration*. 3d ed. Indianapolis, Ind.: JIST Works, 2001) are available at libraries. Electronic versions of the NOC (http://www23.hrdc-drhc. gc.ca) and O*NET-SOC (http://online.onetcenter.org) are available on the World Wide Web. When no DOT, GOE, NOC, or O*NET-SOC numbers are present, this means that the U.S. Department of Labor or Human Resources Development Canada have not created a numerical designation for this career. In this instance, you will see the acronym "N/A," or not available.

The **Overview** section is a brief introductory description of the duties and responsibilities involved in this career. Oftentimes, a career may have a variety of job titles. When this is the case, alternative career titles are presented.

The **History** section describes the history of the particular job as it relates to the overall development of its industry or field.

The **Job** describes the primary and secondary duties of the job.

Requirements discusses high school and postsecondary education and training requirements, any certification or licensing that is necessary, and other personal requirements for success in the job.

Exploring offers suggestions on how to gain experience in or knowledge of the particular job before making a firm educational and financial commitment. The focus is on what can be done while still in high school (or in the early years of college) to gain a better understanding of the job.

The **Employers** section gives an overview of typical places of employment for the job.

Starting Out discusses the best ways to land that first job, be it through the college placement office, newspaper ads, or personal contact.

The **Advancement** section describes what kind of career path to expect from the job and how to get there.

Earnings lists salary ranges and describes the typical fringe benefits.

The **Work Environment** section describes the typical surroundings and conditions of employment—whether indoors or outdoors, noisy or quiet, social or independent. Also discussed are typical hours worked, any seasonal fluctuations, and the stresses and strains of the job.

The **Outlook** section summarizes the job in terms of the general economy and industry projections. For the most part, Outlook information is obtained from the U.S. Bureau of Labor Statistics and is supplemented by information taken from professional associations. Job growth terms follow those used in the *Occupational Outlook Handbook*. Growth described as "much faster than the average" means an increase of 36 percent or more. Growth described as "faster than the average" means an increase of 21 to 35 percent. Growth described as "about as fast as the average" means an increase of 10 to 20 percent. Growth described as "more slowly than the average" means an increase of 3 to 9 percent. Growth described as "little or no change" means an increase of 0 to 2 percent. "Decline" means a decrease of 1 percent or more.

Each article ends with **For More Information,** which lists organizations that provide information on training, education, internships, scholarships, and job placement.

Careers in Focus: Real Estate also includes photos, informative sidebars, and interviews with professionals in the field.

Advertising Workers

QUICK FACTS

School Subjects
English
Psychology
Speech

Personal Skills
Artistic
Communication/ideas

Work Environment
Primarily indoors
Primarily one location

Minimum Education Level
Bachelor's degree

Salary Range
$20,640 to $41,410 to
$500,000

Certification or Licensing
None available

Outlook
About as fast as the average

DOT
131

GOE
10.01.01, 10.02.02

NOC
1122, 5121

O*NET-SOC
11-2011.00, 41-3011.00

OVERVIEW

Advertising is defined as mass communication paid for by an advertiser to persuade a particular segment of the public to adopt ideas or take actions of benefit to the advertiser. *Advertising workers* perform the various creative and business activities needed to take an advertisement from the research stage, to creative concept, through production, and finally to its intended audience. Advertising workers employed in the real estate industry help real estate developers, agents, brokers, and other professionals in the field sell their services or sell or lease residential, commercial, or agricultural property. There are 157,000 advertising sales agents and 85,000 advertising and promotions managers employed in the United States.

HISTORY

Advertising has been around as long as people have been exchanging goods and services. While a number of innovations spurred the development of advertising, it wasn't until the invention of the printing press in the 15th century that merchants began posting handbills in order to advertise their goods and services. By the 19th century, newspapers became an important means of advertising, followed by magazines in the late 1800s.

In the late 1800s, the real estate industry in large eastern cities such as New York and Philadelphia realized the benefits of print advertising and soon began touting all types of properties to the public in newspapers and magazines. For example, real estate advertisements from September 24 to 25, 1887, in *The Philadelphia Press* trumpeted middle class suburban estates that offered fast commute times from country estates to the city ("17 minutes by express trains"), afford-able pricing ("lots from $250 to $1,000"), easy financing ("of $5 to $10 a month"), impressive decor ("elegant fixtures, decorated wall-paper, and otherwise good taste"), and amenities ("supplied with artesian well water and fitted up with sanitary plumbing"). These advertising techniques are quite similar to those used today—with the exception of the improvements in modern-day decor and ameni-ties and the unfortunate increase in price.

One of the problems confronting merchants in the early days of advertising was where to place their ads to generate the most busi-ness. In response, a number of people emerged who specialized in the area of advertising, accepting ads and posting them conspicu-ously. These agents were the first advertising workers. As competi-tion among merchants increased, many of these agents offered to compose ads, as well as post them, for their clients.

Today, with intense competition among both new and existing businesses, advertising has become a necessity in the marketing of goods, property, and services alike. At the same time, the advertis-ing worker's job has grown more demanding and complex than ever. With a wide variety of media from which advertisers can choose—including newspapers, magazines, billboards, radio, television, film and video, the World Wide Web, and a variety of other new tech-nologies—today's advertising worker must not only develop and create ads and campaigns but keep abreast of current and developing buying and technology trends as well.

THE JOB

Approximately seven out of every 10 advertising organizations in the United States are full-service operations, offering their clients a broad range of services, including copywriting, graphics and other art-related work, production, media placement, and tracking and follow-up. These advertising agencies may have hundreds of people working in a dozen different departments, while smaller companies often employ just a handful of employees. Most agencies, however, have at least five departments: contact, research, media, creative, and production.

Contact department personnel are responsible for attracting new customers, and maintaining relationships with existing ones. Heading the contact department, *advertising agency managers* are concerned with the overall activities of the company. They formu-late plans to generate business, by either soliciting new accounts or getting additional business from established clients. In addition, they meet with department heads to coordinate their operations and to create policies and procedures.

Advertising account executives are the contact department employees responsible for maintaining good relations between their clients and the agency. Acting as liaisons, they represent the agency to its clients and must therefore be able to communicate clearly and effectively. After examining the advertising objectives of their clients, account executives develop campaigns or strategies and then work with others from the various agency departments to target specific audiences, create advertising communications, and execute the campaigns. (In the real estate industry, advertising objectives might range from an apartment-finding service seeking to reach people under 30 who are new to the city, to a real estate developer who is interested in educating the public about his affordable, ecofriendly, lakefront condominiums, to a mortgage broker who just opened up shop and needs to educate the public about her services.) Since they present concepts, as well as the ad campaign at various stages of completion, to clients for their feedback and approval, account executives must have some knowledge of overall marketing strategies and be able to sell ideas.

Working with account executives, employees in the research department gather, analyze, and interpret the information needed to make a client's advertising campaign successful. By determining who the potential buyers of a product, property, or service will be, *research workers* predict which theme will have the most impact, what kind of packaging and price will have the most appeal, and which media will be the most effective.

Guided by a *research director,* research workers conduct local, regional, and national surveys in order to examine consumer preferences and then determine potential sales for the targeted product, property, or service based on those preferences. Researchers also gather information about competitors' prices, sales, and advertising methods.

Although research workers often recommend which media to use for an advertising campaign, *media planners* are the specialists who determine which print or broadcast media will be the most effective. Ultimately, they are responsible for choosing the combination of media that will reach the greatest number of potential buyers for the least amount of money, based on their clients' advertising strategies. Accordingly, planners must be familiar with the markets that each medium reaches, as well as the advantages and disadvantages of advertising in each.

Media buyers, often referred to as *space buyers* (for newspapers and magazines), or *time buyers* (for radio and television), do the actual purchasing of space and time according to a general plan formulated by the *media director*. In addition to ensuring that ads appear when and where they should, buyers negotiate costs for ad placement and maintain contact and extensive correspondence with clients and media representatives alike.

While the contact, research, and media departments handle the business side of a client's advertising campaign, the creative staff takes care of the artistic aspects. *Creative directors* oversee the activities of artists and writers and work with clients and account executives to determine the best advertising approaches, gain approval on concepts, and establish budgets and schedules.

Copywriters take the ideas submitted by creative directors and account executives and write descriptive text in the form of headlines, jingles, slogans, and other copy designed to attract the attention of potential buyers. In addition to being able to express themselves clearly and persuasively, copywriters must know what motivates people to buy. For example, they must be able to describe a property's features (e.g., "an easy walk to the lake," "stainless steel appliances," "heated, indoor parking," "central air conditioning," "a rooftop deck with views of the skyline," etc.) or a real estate professional's services and qualifications (e.g., "the lowest interest rates available," "friendly customer service," "over 30 years in the mortgage industry," etc.) in a captivating and appealing way and be familiar with various advertising media. In large agencies, copywriters may be supervised by a *copy chief*.

Copywriters work closely with art directors to make sure that text and artwork create a unified, eye-catching arrangement. Planning the visual presentation of the client's message, from concept formulation to final artwork, the *art director* plays an important role in every stage of the creation of an advertising campaign. Art directors who work on filmed commercials and videos combine film techniques, music, and sound, as well as actors or animation, to communicate an advertiser's message. In publishing, art directors work with graphic designers, photographers, copywriters, and editors to develop brochures, catalogs, direct mail, and other printed pieces, all according to the advertising strategy.

Art directors must have a basic knowledge of graphics and design, computer software, printing, photography, and filmmaking. With the help of graphic artists, they decide where to place text and images, choose typefaces, and create storyboard ads and videos. Several layouts are usually submitted to the client, who chooses one or asks for revisions until a layout or conceptualization sketch meets with final approval. The art director then selects an illustrator, graphic artist, photographer, or TV or video producer, and the project moves on to the production department of the agency.

Production departments in large ad agencies may be divided into print production and broadcast production divisions, each with its own managers and staff. *Production managers* and their assistants convert and reproduce written copy and artwork into printed, filmed, or tape-recorded form so that they can be presented to the public. Production employees work closely with imaging, printing, engraving, and other art reproduction firms and must be familiar with various printing processes, papers, inks, typography, still and motion picture photography, digital imaging, and other processes and materials.

In addition to the principal employees in the five major departments, advertising organizations work with a variety of staff or freelance employees who have specialized knowledge, education, and skill, including photographers, photoengravers, typographers, printers, telemarketers, product and package designers, and producers of display materials. Finally, rounding out most advertising establishments are various support employees, such as *production coordinators, video editors, word processors, statisticians, accountants, administrators, secretaries,* and *clerks.*

The work of advertising employees is fast-paced, dynamic, and ever-changing, depending on each client's strategies and budgets and the creative ideas generated by agency workers. In addition to innovative techniques, methods, media, and materials used by agency workers, new and emerging technologies are impacting the work of everyone in the advertising arena, from marketing executives to graphic designers. The Internet is undoubtedly the most revolutionary medium to hit the advertising scene. Through this worldwide, computer-based network, researchers are able to precisely target markets and clearly identify consumer needs. In addition, the Internet provides media specialists with a powerful vehicle for advertising their clients' products, properties, and services. New technology has also been playing an important role in the creative area. Most art directors, for example, use a variety of computer software programs, and many create and oversee websites for their clients. Other interactive materials and vehicles, such as CD catalogs, touch-screens, and multidimensional visuals, are changing the way today's advertising workers are doing their jobs.

REQUIREMENTS

High School

You can prepare for a career as an advertising worker by taking a variety of courses at the high school level. General liberal arts courses, such as English, journalism, communications, economics, psychology, speech, business, social science, and mathematics, are important for aspiring advertising employees. In addition, those interested in the creative side of the field should take such classes as art, drawing, graphic design, illustration, and art history. Finally, since computers play a vital role in the advertising field, you should become familiar with word processing and layout programs, as well as the World Wide Web.

Postsecondary Training

The American Association of Advertising Agencies notes that most agencies employing entry-level personnel prefer college graduates. Copywriters are best prepared with a college degree in English, journalism, or communications; research workers need college training in statistics, market research, and social studies; and most account executives have degrees in business or a related areas. Media positions are increasingly requiring a college degree in communications or a technology-related area. Media directors and research directors with a master's degree have a distinct advantage over those with only an undergraduate degree. Some research department heads even have doctorates.

While the requirements from agency to agency may vary somewhat, graduates of liberal arts colleges or those with majors in fields such as communications, journalism, business administration, or marketing research are preferred. Good language skills, as well as a broad liberal arts background, are necessary for advertising workers. College students interested in the field should therefore take such courses as English, writing, art, philosophy, foreign languages, social studies, sociology, psychology, economics, mathematics, statistics, advertising, and marketing. If you plan to pursue a career in real estate advertising, it will also help to take some basic real estate courses, which will provide you with an overview of the field. Some 900 degree-granting institutions throughout the United States offer specialized majors in advertising as part of their curriculum.

Other Requirements

In addition to the variety of educational and work experiences necessary for those aspiring to advertising careers, many personal characteristics are also important. Although you will perform many tasks of your job independently as an advertising worker, you will also interact with others as part of a team. In addition to working with other staff members, you may be responsible for initiating and maintaining client contact. You must therefore be able to get along well with people and communicate clearly.

Advertising is not a job that involves routine, and you must be able to meet and adjust to the challenges presented by each new client. The ability to think clearly and logically is important, because commonsense approaches rather than gimmicks persuade people that something is worth buying. You must also be creative, flexible, and imaginative in order to anticipate consumer demand and trends, to develop effective concepts, and to sell the properties or services of your clients.

Finally, with technology evolving at breakneck speed, it's vital that you keep pace with technological advances and trends. In addition to being able to work with the most current software and hardware, you should be familiar with the Web, as well as with other technology that is impacting—and will continue to impact—the industry.

EXPLORING

If you aspire to a career in the advertising industry, you can gain valuable insight by taking writing and art courses offered either in school or by private organizations. In addition to the theoretical ideas and techniques that such classes provide, you can actually apply what you learn by working full or part time at local department stores or newspaper offices. Some advertising agencies or research firms also employ students to interview people or to conduct other market research. Work as an agency clerk or messenger may also be available. Other good employers might include real estate agents, property management companies, and real estate development companies. Participating in internships at an advertising or marketing organization—especially one that specializes in real estate advertising—is yet another way to explore the field, as well as to determine your aptitude for advertising work. You may find it helpful to read publications dedicated to this industry, such as *Advertising Age* (http://www.adage.com).

EMPLOYERS

Most advertising workers are employed by advertising agencies that plan and prepare advertising material for their clients on a commission or service fee basis. However, some large companies and nearly all department stores prefer to handle their own advertising. Advertising workers in such organizations prepare advertising materials for in-house clients, such as the marketing or catalog department.

They also may be involved in the planning, preparation, and production of special promotional materials, such as sales brochures, articles describing the activities of the organization, or websites. Some advertising workers are employed by owners of various media, including newspapers, magazines, radio and television networks, and outdoor advertising. Workers employed in these media are mainly sales representatives who sell advertising space or broadcast time to advertising agencies or companies that maintain their own advertising departments.

Advertising workers who are employed in the real estate industry work for newspapers and magazines that specialize in covering real estate news. In this capacity, they help real estate developers and agents devise advertising campaigns that help lease or sell property. Advertising workers may also work as freelancers, helping mortgage brokers, property and casualty insurance agents, and other real estate professionals advertise their services to the public, businesses, and other organizations.

In addition to agencies, large companies, and department stores, advertising services and supply houses employ such advertising specialists as photographers, photoengravers, typographers, printers, product and package designers, display producers, and others who assist in the production of various advertising materials.

According to the American Association of Advertising Agencies, there are more than 13,000 advertising agencies in the United States. Most of the large firms are located in Chicago, Los Angeles, and New York. Employment opportunities are also available, however, at a variety of "small shops," four out of five of which employ fewer than 10 workers each. In addition, a growing number of self-employment and home-based business opportunities are resulting in a variety of industry jobs located in outlying areas rather than in big cities.

STARTING OUT

Although competition for advertising jobs is fierce and getting your foot in the door can be difficult, there are a variety of ways to launch a career in the field. Some large advertising agencies recruit college graduates and place them in training programs designed to acquaint beginners with all aspects of advertising work, but these opportunities are limited and highly competitive.

Instead, many graduates simply send resumes to businesses that employ entry-level advertising workers. Newspapers, radio and television stations, printers, photographers, and advertising agencies are but a few of the businesses that will hire beginners. The *Standard Directory of Advertising Agencies* (New Providence, N.J.: National Register Publishing Company, 2003) lists the names and addresses of ad agencies all across the nation. You can find the directory in almost any public library.

Those who have had work experience in sales positions often enter the advertising field as account executives. High school graduates and other people without experience who want to work in advertising, however, may find it necessary to begin as clerks or assistants to research and production staff members or to copywriters.

ADVANCEMENT

The career path in an advertising agency generally leads from trainee to skilled worker to division head and then to department head. It may also take employees from department to department, allowing them to gain more responsibility with each move. Opportunities abound for those with talent, leadership capability, and ambition.

Management positions require experience in all aspects of advertising, including agency work, communication with advertisers, and knowledge of various advertising media. Copywriters, account executives, and other advertising agency workers who demonstrate outstanding ability to deal with clients and supervise coworkers usually have a good chance of advancing to management positions. Other workers, however, prefer to acquire specialized skills. For them, advancement may mean more responsibility, the opportunity to perform more specialized tasks, and increased pay.

Advertising workers at firms that have their own advertising departments can also earn promotions. Advancement in any phase of advertising work is usually dependent on the employee's experience, training, and demonstrated skills.

Some qualified copywriters, artists, and account executives establish their own agencies or become marketing consultants. For these entrepreneurs, advancement may take the form of an increasing number of accounts and/or more prestigious clients.

EARNINGS

Salaries of advertising workers vary depending on the type of work, the size of the agency, its geographic location, the kind of accounts handled, and the agency's gross earnings. Salaries are also determined by a worker's education, aptitude, and experience. The wide range of jobs in advertising makes it difficult to estimate average salaries for all positions.

According to a survey by the National Association of Colleges and Employers, marketing majors entering the job market in 2003 had average starting salaries of $34,038, while advertising majors averaged $29,495.

The U.S. Department of Labor reports that the median annual earnings for advertising sales agents in 2004 were $41,410. The lowest paid 10 percent earned less than $20,640, while the highest paid advertising sales agents earned more than $89,290. Advertising sales agents who were employed at newspaper, directory, and book publishers has mean annual earnings of $43,060, while those in radio and television broadcasting earned $49,580.

In advertising agencies, an executive vice president can earn from $113,000 to $500,000 a year or more. Account executives earned a median of $57,000, while senior account executives earned a median of $73,000. In the research and media departments, media directors earn a median of $102,000, and media planners and buyers between $40,000 and $45,000 per year. In the creative department, art directors earn a median of $73,000 or more annually. Salaries for relatively glamorous jobs at agencies can be low, due to high competition. In advertising departments at other businesses and industries, individual earnings vary widely. Salaries of advertising workers are generally higher, however, at consumer product firms than at industrial product organizations because of the competition among consumer product producers. The majority of companies offer insurance benefits, a retirement plan, and other incentives and bonuses.

WORK ENVIRONMENT

Conditions at most agencies are similar to those found in other offices throughout the country, except that employees must frequently work under great pressure to meet deadlines. While a traditional 40-hour workweek is the norm at some companies, almost half (44 percent) of advertising, marketing, promotions, public relations, and sales managers report that they work more hours per week, including evenings and weekends. Bonuses and time off during slow periods are sometimes provided as a means of compensation for unusual workloads and hours.

Although some advertising employees, such as researchers, work independently on a great many tasks, most must function as part of a team. With frequent meetings with coworkers, clients, and media representatives alike, the work environment is usually energized, with ideas being exchanged, contracts being negotiated, and schedules being modified.

Advertising work is fast-paced and exciting. As a result, many employees often feel stressed out as they are constantly challenged to take initiative and be creative. Nevertheless, advertising workers enjoy both professional and personal satisfaction in seeing the culmination of their work communicated to sometimes millions of people.

OUTLOOK

Employment opportunities in the advertising industry is expected to increase slightly faster than the average for all industries through 2012. Demand for advertising workers in the real estate industry will grow as a result of the current strong real estate market, but employment in this specialty may decline if their is a downturn in the real estate market. Network and cable television, radio, newspapers, the Web, and certain other media (particularly interactive vehicles) will offer advertising workers an increasing number of employment opportunities. Some media, such as magazines, direct mail, and event marketing, are expected to provide fewer job opportunities.

Advertising agencies will enjoy faster than average employment growth, as will industries that service ad agencies and other businesses in the advertising field, such as those that offer commercial photography, imaging, art, and graphics services.

At the two extremes, enormous "mega-agencies" and small shops employing up to only 10 workers each offer employment opportunities for people with experience, talent, flexibility, and drive. In addition, self-employment and home-based businesses are on the rise. Many nonindustrial companies, such as banks, schools, and hospitals, will also be creating advertising positions.

In general, openings will become available to replace workers who change positions, retire, or leave the field for other reasons. Competition for these jobs will be keen, however, because of the large number of qualified professionals in this traditionally desirable field. Opportunities will be best for the well-qualified and well-trained applicant. Employers favor college graduates with experience, a high level of creativity, and strong communications skills. People who are not well qualified or prepared for agency work will find the advertising field increasingly difficult to enter. The same is also true for those who seek work in companies that service ad agencies.

FOR MORE INFORMATION

For information on student chapters, scholarships, and internships, contact

American Advertising Federation
1101 Vermont Avenue, NW, Suite 500
Washington, DC 20005-6306
Tel: 202-898-0089
Email: aaf@aaf.org
http://www.aaf.org

For industry information, contact

American Association of Advertising Agencies
405 Lexington, 18th Floor
New York, NY 10174-1801
Tel: 212-682-2500
http://www.aaaa.org

For career and salary information, contact

American Marketing Association
311 South Wacker Drive, Suite 5800
Chicago, IL 60606
Tel: 800-AMA-1150
Email: info@ama.org
http://www.marketingpower.com

The Art Directors Club is an international, nonprofit organization for creative people in advertising, graphic design, interactive media, broadcast design, typography, packaging, environmental design, photography, illustration, and related disciplines.

Art Directors Club
106 West 29th Street
New York, NY 10001
Tel: 212-643-1440
Email: info@adcglobal.org
http://www.adcglobal.org

For information on student membership and careers, contact

Direct Marketing Educational Foundation
1120 Avenue of the Americas
New York, NY 10036-6700
Tel: 212-768-7277
http://www.the-dma.org

The Graphic Artists Guild promotes and protects the economic interests of the artist/designer and is committed to improving conditions for all creators of graphic art and raising standards for the entire industry.

Graphic Artists Guild
90 John Street, Suite 403
New York, NY 10038-3202
Tel: 212-791-3400
http://www.gag.org

Architects

OVERVIEW

Architects plan, design, and observe construction of facilities used for human occupancy and of other structures. They consult with clients, plan layouts of buildings, prepare drawings of proposed buildings, write specifications, and prepare scale and full-sized drawings. Architects also may help clients to obtain bids, select a contractor, and negotiate the construction contract, and they also visit construction sites to ensure that the work is being completed according to specification. There are approximately 92,350 architects working in the United States.

HISTORY

Architecture began not with shelters for people to live in but with the building of religious structures—from Stonehenge in England and the pyramids in Egypt to pagodas in Japan and the Parthenon in Greece. It was the Romans who developed a new building method—concrete vaulting—that made possible large cities with permanent masonry buildings. As they extended the Roman Empire, they built for public and military purposes. They developed and built apartment buildings, law courts, public baths, theaters, and circuses. The industrial revolution—with its demand for factories and mills—led to the development of iron and steel construction, which evolved into the steel and glass skyscraper of today.

Because the history of architecture follows that of human civilization, the architecture of any period reflects the culture of its people. Architecture of early periods has influenced that of later centuries, including the work of contemporary architects. The field continues to develop as new techniques and materials are discovered and as architects blend creativity with function.

THE JOB

The architect normally has two responsibilities: to design a building that will satisfy the client and to protect the public's health, safety, and welfare. This second responsibility requires architects to be licensed by the state in which they work. Meeting the first responsibility involves many steps. The job begins with learning what the client wants. The architect takes many factors into consideration, including local and state building and design regulations, climate, soil on which the building is to be constructed, zoning laws, fire regulations, and the client's financial limitations.

The architect then prepares a set of plans that, upon the client's approval, will be developed into final design and construction documents. The final design shows the exact dimensions of every portion of the building, including the location and size of columns and beams, electrical outlets and fixtures, plumbing, heating and air-conditioning facilities, windows, and doors. The architect works closely with consulting engineers on the specifics of the plumbing, heating, air conditioning, and electrical work to be done.

The architect then assists the client in getting bids from general contractors, one of whom will be selected to construct the building to the specifications. The architect helps the client through the completion of the construction and occupancy phases, making certain the correct materials are used and that the drawings and specifications are faithfully followed.

Throughout the process the architect works closely with a design or project team. This team is usually made up of the following: *designers,* who specialize in design development; a *structural designer,* who designs the frame of the building in accordance with the work of the architect; the *project manager* or *job superintendent,* who sees that the full detail drawings are completed to the satisfaction of the architect; and the *specification writer* and *estimator,* who prepare a project manual that describes in more detail the materials to be used in the building, their quality and method of installation, and all details related to the construction of the building.

The architect's job is very complex. He or she is expected to know construction methods, engineering principles and practices, and materials. Architects also must be up-to-date on new design and construction techniques and procedures. Architects may specialize

Architecture Specialties

Type of Business	Percent of Total Architects Employed
Architecture firms	83
Commercial/industrial/institutional sector	8
Government	3
Design firms	2
Schools	2
Contractor/builder firms	1
Engineering firms	1

Source: American Institute of Architects

in any one of a number of fields, including building appraisal, city planning, teaching, architectural journalism, furniture design, lighting design, or government service. Regardless of the area of specialization, the architect's major task is that of understanding the client's needs and then reconciling them into a meaningful whole.

REQUIREMENTS

High School
To prepare for this career while in high school, take a college preparatory program that includes courses in English, mathematics, physics, art (especially freehand drawing), social studies, history, and foreign languages. Courses in business and computer science also will be useful.

Postsecondary Training
Because most state architecture registration boards require a professional degree, high school students are advised, early in their senior year, to apply for admission to a professional program that is accredited by the National Architectural Accrediting Board (http://www. naab.org). Competition to enter these programs is high. Grades, class rank, and aptitude and achievement scores count heavily in determining who will be accepted.

Most schools of architecture offer degrees through either a five-year bachelor's program or a three- or four-year master's program.

The majority of architecture students seek out the bachelor's degree in architecture, going from high school directly into a five-year program. Though this is the fastest route, you should be certain that you want to study architecture. Because the programs are so specialized, it is difficult to transfer to another field of study if you change your mind. The master's degree option allows for more flexibility but takes longer to complete. In this case, students first earn a liberal arts degree and then continue their training by completing a master's program in architecture.

A typical college architecture program includes courses in architectural history and theory, the technical and legal aspects of building design, science, and liberal arts.

Certification or Licensing

All states and the District of Columbia require that individuals be licensed before contracting to provide architectural services in that particular state. Though many work in the field without licensure, only licensed architects are required to take legal responsibility for all work. Using a licensed architect for a project is, therefore, less risky than using an unlicensed one. Architects who are licensed usually take on projects with larger responsibilities and have greater chances to advance to managerial or executive positions.

The requirements for registration include graduation from an accredited school of architecture and three years of practical experience (called an internship) with a licensed architect. After these requirements are met, individuals can take the rigorous four-day Architect Registration Examination. Some states require architects to maintain their licensing through continued education. These individuals may complete a certain number of credits every year or two through seminars, workshops, university classes, self-study courses, or other sources.

In addition to becoming licensed, a growing number of architects choose to obtain certification by the National Council of Architecture Registration Boards. If an architect plans to work in more than one state, obtaining this certification can make it easier to become licensed in different states.

Other Requirements

If you are interested in architecture, you should be intelligent, observant, responsible, and self-disciplined. You should have a concern for detail and accuracy, be able to communicate effectively both orally and in writing, and be able to accept criticism constructively. Although great artistic ability is not necessary, you should be able to visualize spatial relationships and have the capacity to solve techni-

Architects discuss a project at a construction site. *(Benelux Press/Index Stock Imagery)*

cal problems. Mathematical ability is also important. In addition, you should possess organizational skills and leadership qualities and be able to work well with others.

EXPLORING

Most architects will welcome the opportunity to talk with young people interested in entering architecture. You may be able to visit their offices to gain firsthand knowledge of the type of work architects do. You can also visit a design studio of a school of architecture or work for an architect or building contractor during summer vacations. Also, many architecture schools offer summer programs for high school students. Books and magazines on architecture also can give you a broad understanding of the nature of the work and the values of the profession.

EMPLOYERS

Of the more than 92,000 architects working in the United States, most are employed by architectural firms or other firms related to the construction industry. About one in five architects, however, are self-employed—the ultimate dream of many people in the profession.

A few develop graphic design, interior design, or product specialties. Still others put their training to work in the theater, film, or television fields, or in museums, display firms, and architectural product and materials manufacturing companies. A small number are employed in government agencies such as the Departments of Defense, Interior, and Housing and Urban Development, and the General Services Administration.

STARTING OUT

Students entering architecture following graduation start as interns in an architectural office. As interns, they assist in preparing architectural construction documents. They also handle related details, such as administering contracts, coordinating the work of other professionals on the project, researching building codes and construction materials, and writing specifications. As an alternative to working for an architectural firm, some architecture graduates go into allied fields such as construction, engineering, interior design, landscape architecture, or real estate development.

ADVANCEMENT

Interns and architects alike are given progressively more complex jobs. Architects may advance to supervisory or managerial positions. Some architects become partners in established firms, while others take steps to establish their own practice.

EARNINGS

Architects earned a median annual salary of $61,430 in 2004, according to the U.S. Department of Labor. The lowest paid 10 percent earned less than $38,660 annually, while the highest paid 10 percent earned $103,140 or more.

The American Institute of Architects (AIA) reports that the starting annual salary for graduates of schools of architecture working during their internship before licensing was approximately $30,000 in 2002.

Well-established architects who are partners in an architectural firm or who have their own businesses generally earn much more than salaried employees. According to the AIA, partners in very large firms can earn $132,000 or more a year. Most employers offer such fringe benefits as health insurance, sick and vacation pay, and retirement plans.

WORK ENVIRONMENT

Architects normally work a 40-hour week. There may be a number of times when they will have to work overtime, especially when under pressure to complete an assignment. Self-employed architects work less regular hours and often meet with clients in their homes or offices during the evening. Architects usually work in comfortable offices, but they may spend a considerable amount of time outside the office visiting clients or viewing the progress of a particular job in the field. Their routines usually vary considerably.

OUTLOOK

Employment in the field is expected to grow about as fast as the average through 2012, according to the U.S. Department of Labor. The number of architects needed will depend on the volume of construction. The construction industry is extremely sensitive to fluctuations in the overall economy, and a continued bad economic climate could result in layoffs. On the positive side, employment of architects is not likely to be affected by the growing use of computer technologies. Rather than replacing architects, computers are being used to enhance the architect's work.

Competition for employment will continue to be strong, particularly in prestigious architectural firms. Openings will not be newly created positions but will become available as the workload increases and established architects transfer to other occupations or leave the field.

FOR MORE INFORMATION

To read Careers in Architecture, *visit the AIA's website.*
American Institute of Architects (AIA)
1735 New York Avenue, NW
Washington, DC 20006-5292
Tel: 800-AIA-3837
Email: infocentral@aia.org
http://www.aia.org

For information on careers, education, scholarships, competitions, and student membership opportunities, contact
American Institute of Architecture Students
1735 New York Avenue, NW
Washington, DC 20006-5292

Tel: 202-626-7472
Email: mailbox@aias.org
http://www.aiasnatl.org

For information on architectural education, contact
Association of Collegiate Schools of Architecture
1735 New York Avenue, NW
Washington, DC 20006
Tel: 202-785-2324
Email: info@acsa-arch.org
http://www.acsa-arch.org

For information on certification, contact
National Council of Architecture Registration Boards
1801 K Street, NW, Suite 1100-K
Washington, DC 20006
Tel: 202-783-6500
Email: customerservice@ncarb.org
http://www.ncarb.org

Assessors
and Appraisers

OVERVIEW

Assessors and appraisers collect and interpret data to make judgments about the value, quality, and use of property. Assessors are government officials who evaluate property for the express purpose of determining how much the real estate owner should pay the city or county government in property taxes. Appraisers evaluate the market value of property to help people make decisions about purchases, sales, investments, mortgages, or loans. Rural districts or small towns may have only a few assessors, while large cities or urban counties may have several hundred. Appraisers are especially in demand in large cities but also work in smaller communities. There are approximately 88,000 real estate assessors and appraisers employed in the United States.

HISTORY

Until the 1930s, most assessors and appraisers were lay people using unscientific, informal methods to estimate the value of property. People who were not trained specifically in the field performed appraisals as a part-time adjunct to a general real estate business. As a result, the "boom" period of the 1920s saw many abuses of appraisals, such as approving loans in excess of the property's real value based on inaccurate estimates. The events of the Great Depression in the 1930s further highlighted the need for professionalism in appraising. Real estate owners defaulted on their mortgages, real estate bond issues stopped paying interest, and real estate corporations went into receivership.

In 1922 the National Association of Real Estate Boards (NAREB) defined specializations of its real estate functions to encourage professionalism in the industry. They did not organize an independent appraisal division, however, because there were few appraisers and the industry at large did not appreciate the importance of sound appraisals.

The NAREB recognized appraising as a significant branch of specialization in 1928 but did not formulate clearly defined appraisal standards and appraisal treatises until the 1930s.

Since then, appraising has emerged as a complex profession offering many responsibilities and opportunities. With the advent of computers, assessing and appraising have become more scientific. Today, assessments are based on a combination of economic and statistical analysis and common sense.

People need reliable appraisals when selling, mortgaging, taxing, insuring, or developing real estate. Buyers and sellers of property want to know the property's market value as a guide in their negotiations and may need economic feasibility studies or advice about other investment considerations for a proposed or existing development. Mortgage lenders require appraisals before issuing loans, and insurance companies often need an estimate of value before underwriting a property.

THE JOB

Property is divided into two distinct types: real property and personal property. Real property is land and the structures built upon the land, while personal property includes all other types of possessions. Appraisers determine the value, quality, and use of real property and personal property based on selective research into market areas, the application of analytical techniques, and professional judgment derived from experience. In evaluating real property, they analyze the supply and demand for different types of property, such as residential dwellings, office buildings, shopping centers, industrial sites, and farms, to estimate their values. Appraisers analyze construction, condition, and functional design. They review public records of sales, leases, previous assessments, and other transactions pertaining to land and buildings to determine the market values, rents, and construction costs of similar properties. Appraisers collect information about neighborhoods, such as availability of gas, electricity, power lines, and transportation. They also may interview people familiar with the property, and they consider the cost of making improvements on the property.

Appraisers also must consider such factors as location and changes that might influence the future value of the property. A residence worth $300,000 in the suburbs may be worth only a fraction of that in the inner city or in a remote rural area. But that same suburban residence may depreciate in value if an airport will be built nearby. After conducting a thorough investigation, appraisers usually prepare a written report that documents their findings and conclusions.

Assessors perform the same duties as appraisers and then compute the amount of tax to be levied on property, using applicable tax tables. The primary responsibility of the assessor is to prepare an annual assessment roll, which lists all properties in a district and their assessed values.

To prepare the assessment roll, assessors and their staffs first must locate and identify all taxable property in the district. To do so, they prepare and maintain complete and accurate maps that show the size, shape, location, and legal description of each parcel of land. Next, they collect information about other features, such as zoning, soil characteristics, and availability of water, electricity, sewers, gas, and telephones. They describe each building and how land and buildings are used. This information is put in a parcel record.

Assessors also analyze relationships between property characteristics and sales prices, rents, and construction costs to produce valuation models or formulas. They use these formulas to estimate the value of every property as of the legally required assessment date. For example, assessors try to estimate the value of adding a bedroom to a residence or adding an acre to a farm, or how much competition from a new shopping center detracts from the value of a downtown department store. Finally, assessors prepare and certify an assessment roll listing all properties, owners, and assessed values and notify owners of the assessed value of their properties. Because taxpayers have the right to contest their assessments, assessors must be prepared to defend their estimates and methods.

Most appraisers deal with land and buildings, but some evaluate other items of value. Specialized appraisers evaluate antiques, gems and jewelry, machinery, equipment, aircraft, boats, oil and gas reserves, and businesses. These appraisers obtain special training in their areas of expertise but generally perform the same functions as real property appraisers.

Personal property assessors help the government levy taxes by preparing lists of personal property owned by businesses and, in a

Earnings by Specialty, 2004

Industry	Employment	Mean Annual Earnings
Local government	24,260	$41,190
Activities related to real estate	23,410	$55,950
State government	2,930	$46,720
Offices of real estate agents and brokers	2,320	$68,370
Nondepository credit intermediation companies	1,630	$53,690
Federal government	650	$73,660
Management and technical consulting service companies	250	$90,590

Source: U.S. Department of Labor

few areas, householders. In addition to listing the number of items, these assessors also estimate the value of taxable items.

REQUIREMENTS

High School

If you are interested in the fields of assessing or appraising, there are a number of courses you can take in high school to help prepare you for this work. Take plenty of math classes, since you will need to be comfortable working with numbers and making calculations. Accounting classes will also be helpful for the same reasons. English courses will help you develop your researching and writing skills as well as verbal skills. Take computer classes in order to become accustomed to using this tool. Courses in civics or government may also be beneficial.

Postsecondary Training

Appraisers and assessors need a broad range of knowledge in such areas as equity and mortgage finance, architectural function, demographic statistics, and business trends. In addition, they must be competent writers and able to communicate effectively with people. In the past, some people have been able to enter these fields with only a high school education and learn specialized skills on the job. Today, however, most appraisers and assessors have at least some college education. A number work in appropriate businesses, such as auction houses, while they earn their degrees. Some with several years of college experience are able to find employment and receive on-the-job training. Those wanting to receive professional designations and to have the best job opportunities, however, should complete a college degree.

A few colleges and universities, such as Lindenwood University (http://www.lindenwood.edu) in St. Charles, Missouri, now offer degrees in valuation sciences that will prepare you for this career. If you are unable to attend such a specialized program, though, there are numerous classes you can take at any college to prepare for this career. A liberal arts degree provides a solid background, as do courses in finance, statistics, mathematics, public administration and business administration, real estate and urban land economics, engineering, architecture, and computer science. Appraisers choosing to specialize in a particular area should have a solid background in that field.

Courses in assessment and appraisal are offered by professional associations such as the American Society of Appraisers (ASA), the Appraisal Institute (AI), and the International Association of Assessing Officers.

Certification or Licensing

A number of professional organizations, such as the ASA and the AI, offer certification or designations in the field. It is highly recommended that you attain professional designation in order to enhance your standing in the field and demonstrate to consumers your level of expertise. To receive a designation, you will typically need to pass a written exam, demonstrate ethical behavior, and have completed a certain amount of education. To maintain your designation, you will also need to fulfill continuing education requirements.

Because all appraisals used for federally regulated real estate transactions must be conducted by licensed appraisers, most appraisers now obtain a state license. In addition, some states—known as "mandatory states"—require real estate appraisers to be licensed even if the appraisers do not deal with federally regulated transactions. You will need to check with your state's regulatory agency to learn more about the exact requirements for your state. In addition to a license, some states may require assessors who are government employees to pass civil service tests or other examinations before they can start work.

Other Requirements

Good appraisers are skilled investigators and must be proficient at gathering data. They must be familiar with sources of information on such diverse topics as public records, construction materials, building trends, economic trends, and governmental regulations affecting use of property. They should know how to read survey drawings and blueprints and be able to identify features of building construction.

EXPLORING

One simple way you can practice the methods used by appraisers is to write a detailed analysis of something you are considering investing in, such as a car, a computer, or even which college to attend. Your analysis should include both the benefits and the shortcomings of the investment as well as your final recommendation. Is the car overpriced? Does one particular school offer a better value for you? By doing this, you will begin to get a feel for the researching and writing done by an appraiser. Another way to explore this career is to look for part-time or summer work with an appraisal firm. Some firms also have jobs as appraiser assistants or trainees. Working at county assessors' or treasurers' offices, financial institutions, or real estate companies also might provide experience. If you are interested in working with real estate, you may want to learn the particulars of building construction by finding summer work with a construction company.

EMPLOYERS

Assessors are public servants who are either elected or appointed to office. The United States is divided into assessment districts, with population size affecting the number of assessors in a given area. Appraisers are employed by private businesses, such as accounting firms, real estate companies, and financial institutions, and by larger assessors' offices. Appraisers also work at auction houses, art galleries, and antique shops; some also work in government offices or for U.S. Customs and Border Protection. Assessors' offices might employ administrators, property appraisers, mappers, systems analysts, computer technicians, public relations specialists, word processors, and clerical workers. In small offices, one or two people might handle most tasks; in large offices, some with hundreds of employees, specialists are more common. Approximately 88,000 real estate assessors and appraisers are employed in the United States.

STARTING OUT

After you have acquired the necessary technical and mathematical knowledge in the classroom, you should apply to area appraisal firms, local county assessors, real estate brokers, or large accounting firms. Because assessing jobs are often civil service positions, they may be listed with government employment agencies. If you have graduated from a degree program in valuation sciences, your school's career services office should also be able to provide you with assistance in finding that first job.

ADVANCEMENT

Appraising is a dynamic field, affected yearly by new legislation and technology. To distinguish themselves in the business, top appraisers continue their education and pursue certification through the various national appraising organizations, such as the Appraisal Institute, the American Society of Appraisers, and the International Association of Assessing Officers. Certified appraisers are entrusted with the most prestigious projects and can command the highest fees. In addition to working on more and more prestigious projects, some appraisers advance by opening their own appraisal firms. Others may advance by moving to larger firms or agency offices, where they are more able to specialize.

EARNINGS

Income for assessors is influenced by their location and employer; their salaries generally increase as the population of their jurisdiction increases. For example, those working in large counties, such as Los Angeles County, may make up to $100,000 annually. Appraisers employed in the private sector tend to earn higher incomes than those in the public sector.

According to a recent survey by *Appraisal Today,* the average annual income of all appraisers is $58,132. Salaries range from $12,500 to $225,000.

The average fee for appraisal of a standard residential property is about $300, but fees can range from $75 for a re-inspection of new construction or repairs to $600 for inspection of a small residential income property.

According to the U.S. Department of Labor, real estate appraisers and assessors earned a median salary of $43,790 in 2004. The lowest paid 10 percent earned $22,820 or less per year on average, while the highest paid earned $83,840 or more.

Earnings at any level are enhanced by higher education and professional designations. Fringe benefits for both public and private employees usually include paid vacations and health insurance.

WORK ENVIRONMENT

Appraisers and assessors have a variety of working conditions, from the comfortable offices where they write and edit appraisal reports to outdoor construction sites, which they visit in both the heat of summer and the bitter cold of winter. Many appraisers spend mornings at their desks and afternoons in the field. Experienced appraisers may need to travel out of state.

Appraisers and assessors who work for a government agency or financial institution usually work 40-hour weeks, with overtime when necessary. Independent appraisers often can set their own schedules.

Appraisal is a very people-oriented occupation. Appraisers must be unfailingly cordial, and they have to deal calmly and tactfully with people who challenge their decisions (and are usually angry). Appraising can be a high-stress occupation because a considerable amount of money and important personal decisions ride on appraisers' calculations.

OUTLOOK

The U.S. Department of Labor estimates that employment of assessors and appraisers will grow about as fast as the average for all occupations through 2012. In general, assessors work in a fairly secure field. As long as governments levy property taxes, assessors will be needed to provide them with information. The real estate industry, however, is influenced dramatically by the overall health of the economy, so appraisers in real estate can expect to benefit during periods of growth and experience slowdowns during recessions and depressions.

FOR MORE INFORMATION

For information on education and professional designations, contact
American Society of Appraisers
555 Herndon Parkway, Suite 125
Herndon, VA 20170
Tel: 703-478-2228
Email: asainfo@appraisers.org
http://www.appraisers.org

Visit this organization's website for a listing of state real estate appraiser regulatory boards.

Appraisal Foundation
1029 Vermont Avenue, NW, Suite 900
Washington, DC 20005-3517
Tel: 202-347-7722
Email: info@appraisalfoundation.org
http://www.appraisalfoundation.org

For information on professional designations, education, careers, and scholarships, contact

Appraisal Institute
550 West Van Buren Street, Suite 1000
Chicago, IL 60607
Tel: 312-335-4100
http://www.appraisalinstitute.org

For information on professional designations, education, and publications, contact

International Association of Assessing Officers
314 West 10th Street
Kansas City, MO 64105-1616
Tel: 816-701-8100
http://www.iaao.org

For information on education and appraisal careers, contact

National Association of Independent Fee Appraisers
401 North Michigan Avenue, Suite 2200
Chicago, IL 60611
Tel: 312-321-6830
Email: info@naifa.com
http://www.naifa.com

INTERVIEW

Michael Evans is the president of Evans Appraisal Service Inc. in Chico, California. He has been an appraiser for 23 years. Michael discussed his career with the editors of Careers in Focus: Real Estate.

Q. Why did you decide to become an appraiser?

A. I didn't know it, but I was trained as a child. My father was an appraiser, and I used to go with him a lot. I learned far more than I ever thought I did. After college, I worked several jobs before coming back home and starting the most interesting and satisfying job I have ever had—one that I plan to do until the day I die!

Q. What are your typical tasks/responsibilities as an appraiser?

A. Valuing real property. We have a diversified office. We handle agricultural, commercial, industrial, residential, and special-purpose properties. Real property appraisal tasks include researching, inspecting, and analyzing the properties being valued, as well as the comparable sales and rental comparables.

Q. What advice would you give to high school students who are interested in this career?

A. A strong background in math and economics is a great help. Most of the education for this field starts at the college level. A business, finance, or accounting degree would be a big plus.

Q. What are the three most important professional qualities for appraisers?

A. Honesty, knowing when to ask for help, and a quality appraisal education like the American Society of Appraisers provides its members.

Q. What is the future employment outlook for appraisers?

A. Many in my field (real property appraisal) believe that the appraisal profession will be shrinking due to the advent of the computer and automated valuation models. My experience has been just the opposite as my business has tripled in the last 10 years. I see more and more need for quality appraisers (like members of the American Society of Appraisers) to perform more in-depth inspections and analysis of properties into the future.

Clerks

OVERVIEW

Clerks perform a variety of clerical tasks that help real estate–related businesses run smoothly, including maintaining files; sorting mail; drafting correspondence; keeping records; typing; answering telephones; taking messages; making photocopies; preparing mailings; computing, classifying, recording, and verifying financial data; and producing and processing bills and collecting payments from customers. In large companies, clerks might have specialized tasks such as inputting data into a computer, but in most cases, clerks are flexible and have many duties. Clerks usually work under close supervision, often with experienced clerks directing their activities.

HISTORY

Before the 18th century, many businesspeople did their own office work, such as shipping products, accepting payments, and recording inventory. The industrial revolution changed the nature of business by popularizing the specialization of labor, which allowed companies to increase their output dramatically. At this time, clerks were brought in to handle the growing amount of clerical duties.

Office workers have become more important as computers, word processors, and other technological advances have increased both the volume of business information available and the speed with which administrative decisions can be made. The number of office workers in the United States has grown as more trained personnel are needed to handle the volume of business communication and information. Businesses (including those in the real estate industry) and government agencies depend on skilled

School Subjects
Business
English
Mathematics

Personal Skills
Communication/ideas
Following instructions

Work Environment
Primarily indoors
Primarily one location

Minimum Education Level
High school diploma

Salary Range
$14,560 to $22,980 to $36,260

Certification or Licensing
None available

Outlook
About as fast as the average

DOT
209

GOE
09.07.02

NOC
1411

O*NET-SOC
43-9061.00

office workers to file and sort documents, operate office equipment, and cooperate with others to ensure the flow of information.

THE JOB

Clerks usually perform a variety of tasks as part of their overall job responsibilities. They may type or file bills, rent or mortgage statements, and business correspondence. They may stuff envelopes, answer telephone calls about available properties or a need for services, and sort mail. Clerks also enter data into computer databases, run errands, and operate office equipment such as photocopiers, fax machines, and switchboards. In the course of an average day, a clerk usually performs a combination of these and other clerical tasks, spending an hour or so on one task and then moving on to another as directed by an office manager or other supervisor.

A clerk may work with other office personnel, such as a bookkeeper or accountant, to maintain a company's financial records. The clerk may type and mail invoices and sort payments as they come in, keep payroll records, or take inventories. With more experience, the clerk may be asked to update customer files to reflect receipt of payments and verify records for accuracy.

Clerks often deliver messages from one office worker to another, an especially important responsibility in larger companies. Clerks may relay questions and answers from one department head to another. Similarly, clerks may relay messages from people outside the company or employees who are outside of the office to those working in house. Clerks may also work with other personnel on individual projects, such as preparing a yearly budget or making sure a mass mailing gets out on time.

The following paragraphs detail the specialties available for people who work as clerks.

Administrative clerks assist in the efficient operation of an office by compiling business records; providing information to sales personnel and customers; and preparing and sending out bills, policies, invoices, and other business correspondence. Administrative clerks may also keep financial records and prepare the payroll.

File clerks review and classify letters, documents, articles, and other information and then file this material so it can be quickly retrieved at a later time. They contribute to the smooth distribution of information at a company.

Billing clerks are responsible for keeping records and up-to-date accounts of all business transactions. They type and send bills for services or products and update files to reflect payments. They also review incoming invoices to ensure that the requested products have been delivered and that the billing statements are accurate and paid on time.

Bookkeeping clerks keep systematic records and current accounts of financial transactions for businesses (such as real estate management companies, developers, and banks), institutions, industries, charities, and other organizations. The bookkeeping records of a firm or business are a vital part of its operational procedures because these records reflect the assets and the liabilities, as well as the profits and losses, of the operation.

REQUIREMENTS

High School
To prepare for a career as a clerk, you should take courses in English, mathematics, and as many business-related subjects, such as keyboarding and bookkeeping, as possible. Community colleges and vocational schools often offer business education courses that provide training for general office workers.

Postsecondary Training
A high school diploma is usually sufficient for beginning clerks, although business courses covering office machine operation and bookkeeping are also helpful. To succeed in this field, you should have computer skills, the ability to concentrate for long periods of time on repetitive tasks, good English and communication skills, and mathematical abilities. Legible handwriting is also a necessity.

Other Requirements
To find work as a clerk, you should have an even temperament, strong communication skills, and the ability to work well with others. You should find systematic and detailed work appealing. Other personal qualifications include dependability, trustworthiness, and a neat personal appearance.

EXPLORING

You can gain experience by taking on clerical or bookkeeping responsibilities with a school club or other organization. In addition, some school work-study programs may provide opportunities for part-time on-the-job training with local businesses, such as real estate agencies, newspapers and magazines that focus on the real estate industry, law firms that specialize in real estate, and financial institutions. You may also be able to get a part-time or summer job in a business office by contacting businesses directly or enlisting the aid of a guidance counselor. Training in the operation of business machinery (computers, word processors, and so on) may be available through evening courses offered by business schools and community colleges.

EMPLOYERS

Major employers include finance and insurance companies, advertising agencies, real estate agencies, local government, health care and social assistance organizations, administrative and support services companies, or professional, scientific, and technical services industries. Smaller companies also hire office workers and sometimes offer a greater opportunity to gain experience in a variety of clerical tasks.

STARTING OUT

To secure an entry-level position, you should contact businesses or government agencies directly. Newspaper ads and temporary-work agencies are also good sources for finding jobs in this area. Most companies provide on-the-job training, during which company policies and procedures are explained.

ADVANCEMENT

Clerks usually begin their employment performing more routine tasks such as delivering messages and sorting and filing mail. With experience, they may advance to more complicated assignments and assume a greater responsibility for the entire project to be completed. Those who demonstrate the desire and ability may move to other clerical positions, such as secretary or receptionist. Clerks with good leadership skills may become group managers or supervisors. To be promoted to a professional occupation such as accountant, a college degree or other specialized training is usually necessary.

The high turnover rate that exists among clerks increases promotional opportunities. The number and kind of opportunities, however, usually depend on the place of employment and the ability, education, and experience of the employee.

EARNINGS

Salaries for clerks vary depending on the size and geographic location of the company and the skills of the worker. According to the

U.S. Department of Labor, the median salary for full-time office clerks was $22,980 in 2004. The lowest paid 10 percent earned less than $14,560, while the highest paid group earned more than $36,260.

According to a 2004 salary survey by OfficeTeam, entry-level office assistants earned between $20,250 and $24,250, while senior office assistants earned up to $32,750.

Full-time workers generally also receive paid vacations, health insurance, sick leave, and other benefits.

WORK ENVIRONMENT

As is the case with most office workers, clerks work an average 37- to 40-hour week. Clerks in the real estate industry may work evenings and weekends, as much of the business conducted in this field occurs during nontraditional business hours. Clerks usually work in comfortable surroundings and are provided with modern equipment. Although clerks have a variety of tasks and responsibilities, the job itself can be fairly routine and repetitive. Clerks often interact with accountants and other office personnel and may work under close supervision.

OUTLOOK

Although employment of clerks is expected to grow only about as fast as the average through 2012, there will still be many jobs available due to the vastness of this field and a high turnover rate. With the increased use of data processing equipment and other types of automated office machinery, more and more employers are hiring people proficient in a variety of office tasks. According to OfficeTeam, the following industries show the strongest demand for qualified administrative staff: mortgage and title, health care, and nonprofits. Other industries that will provide good opportunities include construction, technology, and transportation.

Because they are so versatile, office workers can find employment in virtually any kind of industry, so their overall employment does not depend on the fortunes of any single sector of the economy. In addition to private companies, the federal government should continue to be a good source of jobs. Employment opportunities should be especially good for those trained in various computer skills as well as other office machinery. Temporary and part-time work opportunities should also increase, especially during busy business periods.

FOR MORE INFORMATION

For information on seminars, conferences, and news on the industry, contact

National Association of Executive Secretaries and Administrative Assistants
900 South Washington Street, Suite G-13
Falls Church, VA 22046
Tel: 703-237-8616
Email: headquarters@naesaa.com
http://www.naesaa.com

For information on the real estate industry, contact
National Association of Realtors
430 North Michigan Avenue
Chicago, IL 60611
Tel: 312-329-8292
http://www.realtor.org

For free office career and salary information and job listings, visit the following website:
OfficeTeam
Tel: 800-804-8367
http://www.officeteam.com

Financial Institution Loan Officers and Counselors

OVERVIEW

Loan officers assist individuals or businesses secure loans from financial institutions. They screen potential clients and assist them in the paperwork needed to apply for a loan. Loan officers gather personal and credit information, and use this information to gauge the chance of loan repayment. They may specialize in commercial, consumer, or mortgage loans. *Loan counselors* provide guidance to those individuals or businesses that have qualification problems. In such cases, they may suggest appropriate loans and explain any special requirements or restrictions. Loan officers and counselors may work for banks, mortgage companies, or credit unions. In some institutions, loan officers and counselors may have interchangeable duties. There are approximately 255,000 loan officers and counselors employed in the United States.

HISTORY

The first bank of the United States, the Bank of North America, was chartered by the Continental Congress in 1781. It was established to print money, purchase securities (stocks and bonds) in companies, and lend money. It was at this time that the career of financial institution loan officer and counselor originated—although these tasks were probably handled by the bank owner or his family.

QUICK FACTS

School Subjects
Business
Mathematics

Personal Skills
Communication/ideas
Leadership/management

Work Environment
Primarily indoors
Primarily one location

Minimum Education Level
Bachelor's degree

Salary Range
$24,090 to $49,180 to $102,830

Certification or Licensing
Recommended

Outlook
About as fast as the average

DOT
186

GOE
13.02.04

NOC
0122

O*NET-SOC
13-2071.00, 13-2072.00

More than 220 years later, loan officers and counselors continue to play a key role in the banking industry, overseeing trillions of dollars of commercial, consumer, and mortgage loans. Technology has changed the way loan officers and counselors do their jobs. Today, customers can learn about loan options and be pre-approved for loans via the Internet, and loan officers and counselors use computers, databases, email, and other technology to make the loan process easier for consumers. The number of banks and other financial institutions has grown extensively in the past 25 years, and loan officers and counselors will continue to be needed to help run the banking industry.

THE JOB

For most people, financial loans are necessary to make major purchases such as an automobile or house, construction or renovation of an existing home, or to finance a college education. Companies often take out loans to set up a new business, or gain capital to expand an established business. They turn to different financial institutions such as banks, credit unions, or mortgage companies. Loan officers and counselors act as liaisons for the financial institution and the client.

Loan officers may specialize in commercial, consumer, or business loans, or, depending on the size of the lender, handle all types of loans. The loan process usually starts with an initial interview between the loan officer and client. At this time, the type and size of loan is determined. The loan officer then gathers personal information necessary to complete the application, such as the client's educational background, work history, assets, and credit history. The credit history is important because it often gauges the client's ability to repay the loan. Loan officers can obtain a computerized credit "score" from several reliable sources. If the loan officer is working with a commercial loan, they must also gather the company's financial statements.

Once the information is gathered and verified to be true, then the loan officer meets with a loan manager and/or loan underwriter to determine if the loan should be granted or denied. Upon approval, the loan officer notifies the client and sets up a repayment schedule, or in cases of a mortgage loan, a closing time.

Loan counselors work with clients or businesses that may have problems qualifying for a loan. They find alternate types of loans to best fit the needs of the client, and explain any restrictions or special requirements. They may also help the client set up collateral in order to qualify for the loan. For example, in order to approve a new business loan, the lender may ask the client to offer a home or other asset

A financial institution loan counselor (left) discusses loan options with a customer. *(Jon Riley, Index Stock Imagery)*

as collateral in case they fail to repay the loan. Upon default of the loan, the asset may be sold in order to fulfill repayment.

Frequently, loan officers and loan counselors may have many responsibilities that overlap. This is especially true in cases of smaller lending institutions. Loan officers and counselors often act as salespeople. They may make cold calls, or act on sales leads in order to attract new business. Some loan officers, especially those who specialize in consumer loans, may have established relationships with their clients, often working to secure additional loans as the business grows.

Loan officers and counselors have to keep abreast of new developments in the industry. Depending on their training and experience, they may study potential loan markets to develop loan prospects. They also have to learn new computer software used to obtain credit history, be aware of any new tax laws regarding loans, and take sales training or certification classes as required by their place of employment.

REQUIREMENTS
High School
You will need at least a bachelor's degree if you want to work as a loan officer or counselor. While you are in high school, therefore,

you should take classes that will give you a solid preparation for college. Such classes include mathematics, such as algebra and geometry, science, history, and a foreign language. Take English courses to improve your researching, writing, and communication skills. Also, take computer classes. Computer technology is an integral part of today's financial world, and you will benefit from being familiar with this tool. Finally, if your high school offers classes in economics, accounting, or finance, be sure to take these courses. The course work will not only give you an opportunity to gain knowledge but will also allow you to see if you enjoy working with numbers and theories.

Postsecondary Training

Possible majors for you in college include accounting, economics, finance, or business administration with an emphasis on accounting or finance. You will need to continue honing your computer skills during this time. Also, you will probably have exposure to business law classes. It is important for you to realize that federal and state laws regarding business and finances change, so you will need to familiarize yourself with current regulations.

Many financial management and banking associations offer continuing education programs in conjunction with colleges or universities. These programs are geared toward advancing and updating your knowledge of subjects such as changing banking regulations, financial analysis, and consumer and mortgage lending.

Certification or Licensing

Certification is one way to show your commitment to the field, improve your skills, and increase your possibilities for advancement. The Mortgage Bankers Association offers the certified mortgage banker designation, which has the following areas of expertise: master certified mortgage banker, residential certified mortgage banker, and commercial certified mortgage banker. The association also offers the following specialist designations: accredited mortgage professional, certified mortgage servicer, certified mortgage technologist, certified quality assurance professional, certified residential originator, and certified residential underwriter. The National Association of Credit Management offers business credit professionals a three-part certification program that consists of work experience and examinations. Financial managers pass through the level of credit business associate to credit business fellow to certified credit executive.

Other Requirements

In the banking business, the ability to get along well with others is essential. You should be able to show tact and convey a feeling of understanding and confidence. Honesty is perhaps the most important qualification for this job. Loan officers and counselors have access to confidential financial information about the individuals and business concerns associated with their institutions. Therefore, if you are interested in this career, you must have a high degree of personal integrity.

EXPLORING

Except for high school courses that are business oriented, you will find few opportunities for experience and exploration during high school. Ask your teacher or guidance counselor to arrange a class tour of a financial institution. This will at least give you a taste of how banking services work. You can gain the most valuable experience by finding a part-time or a summer job in a bank or other institution that sometimes hires qualified high school or college students. Finally, to gain some hands-on experience with managing money, consider joining a school or local club in which you could work as the treasurer.

EMPLOYERS

There are approximately 224,000 loan officers and 31,000 loan counselors in the United States. They primarily work for commercial banks, savings institutions, credit unions, and mortgage and consumer finance companies.

STARTING OUT

One way to enter banking as a regular employee is through part-time or summer employment. Anyone can apply for a position by writing to a financial institution officer in charge of personnel or by arranging for an interview appointment. Many institutions advertise in the classified section of local newspapers. The larger banks recruit on college campuses. An officer will visit a campus and conduct interviews at that time. Student career services offices can also arrange interviews.

ADVANCEMENT

There is no one method for advancement among loan officers and counselors. Advancement depends on the size of the institution, the services it offers, and the qualifications of the employee. Usually, the smaller the employer the slower the advancements.

Financial institutions often offer special training programs that take place at night, during the summer, and in some special instances during scheduled working hours. People who take advantage of these opportunities usually find that advancement comes more quickly. The American Banking Institute (part of the American Bankers Association), for example, offers training in every phase of banking through its own facilities or the facilities of the local universities and banking organizations. The length of this training may vary from six months to two years. Years of service and experience are required for a top-level financial institution officer to become acquainted with policy, operations, customers, and the community. Similarly, the National Association of Credit Management offers training and instruction.

EARNINGS

Those who enter banking in the next few years will find their earnings to be dependent on their experience, the size of the institution, and its location. In general, starting salaries in financial institutions are not usually the highest, although among larger financial institutions in big cities, starting salaries often compare favorably with salaries in large corporations.

Loan officers earned median annual salaries of $49,180 in 2004, according to the U.S. Department of Labor. The lowest paid 10 percent of loan officers made approximately $28,190, while the highest paid 10 percent earned $102,830 or more. Loan counselors earned salaries that ranged from less than $24,090 to $63,200 or more in 2004.

Group life insurance, paid vacations, profit-sharing plans, and health care and retirement plans are some of the benefits offered to loan officers and counselors.

WORK ENVIRONMENT

Working conditions in financial institutions are generally pleasant. They are usually clean, well maintained, and often air-conditioned. They are generally located throughout cities for the convenience of both customers and employees. Working hours for financial institution loan officers and counselors may be somewhat irregular, as many organizations have expanded their hours of business.

OUTLOOK

The number of job openings for loan officers and counselors is expected to increase about as fast as the average for all other occupations through 2012, according to predictions by the U.S. Department of Labor. College graduates, or those with work experience in lending, banking, or sales, will have the best employment opportunities.

A healthy economy has created a great demand for new or refinanced mortgage loans, construction loans, home equity loans, and business loans. The boom in the real estate market created many job openings for loan officers and counselors to meet the demand. However, this industry is closely tied to the nation's economic status. High unemployment, or higher interest rates may make the public wary of taking on unnecessary financial obligations. This could result in fewer employment opportunities for loan officers and counselors. Since most loan officers work on commission, a drastic change in the real estate market would dramatically change their earning potential.

Advances in the way people apply for loans could also spell employment woes. While computerized credit scoring, online mortgage shopping, and online loan applications may increase the efficiency of a loan officer, unfortunately they may also cut the number professionals needed to get the job done.

FOR MORE INFORMATION

This organization has information about the banking industry and continuing education available through the American Institute of Banking. It also has information on the Stonier Graduate School of Banking.

American Bankers Association
1120 Connecticut Avenue, NW
Washington, DC 20036
Tel: 800-226-5377
http://www.aba.com

For certification, industry news, and career information, contact
Association for Financial Professionals
7315 Wisconsin Avenue, Suite 600 West
Bethesda, MD 20814
Tel: 301-907-2862
http://www.afponline.org

For information on education, certification, and employment opportunities, contact
Mortgage Bankers Association of America
1919 Pennsylvania Avenue, NW
Washington, DC 20006-3438
Tel: 202-557-2700
http://www.mbaa.org

For information on certification, continuing education, and general information on the banking and credit industry, contact
National Association of Credit Management
8840 Columbia 100 Parkway
Columbia, MD 21045
Tel: 410-740-5560
Email: nacm_info@nacm.org
http://www.nacm.org

INTERVIEW

Matt Bryant is a mortgage broker at Prime Mortgage Bancshares in Chicago, Illinois. He has worked in the field since June 2002. Matt discussed his career with the editors of Careers in Focus: Real Estate.

Q. Why did you decide to become a mortgage broker?

A. In the summer of 2002, I was actively seeking new employment. One of my good friends as well as another acquaintance were both working as mortgage brokers. I took a job as a loan processor for my good friend, working as a broker myself for any loans that I could generate on my own (but working mainly as his loan processor). This was in the middle of the refinance boom, and my friend was so busy he couldn't keep up. He told me that the best way to learn the loan process and see if I wanted to become a broker was to process loans for him (for a nice fee) and learn how the process worked. And then if I liked it, I would have a position working as a fellow broker for his employer, Prime Mortgage Bancshares. It took about a month (our agreement was for six months), and I knew that I wanted to become a broker as a career for myself.

Q. What are your typical tasks/responsibilities as a mortgage broker?

A. As a broker, my main responsibility is collecting information from potential borrowers, and then analyzing all the information to determine the best possible loan program for that specific borrower. It's very important to try and get as much information as you can from each person so that you can make an educated assessment of what they need and fit the best loan to their specific wants/needs. Once a loan program is picked out and the borrower decides to move forward, then my responsibilities shift from more of a consulting role to more action. I've got to do everything that is involved with closing a loan in an efficient manner so that the loan can close as scheduled. Another big responsibility is keeping your customers informed and educated throughout the entire loan process. You want to make sure that they are completely satisfied with your service so they will want to use you again in the future and/or refer others to your business. It's very important that they feel extremely confident that you have done right for them.

Q. What advice would you give to high school students who are interested in this career?

A. Polish your math skills. The mortgage business is very math specific. I also think that you need to be a helpful person. The great thing about my job is that there is always a very visible beginning, middle, and end. The beginning is the information gathering that I discussed earlier. The middle is all the work to do on the loan. The end is the closing and customer satisfaction. My favorite part about my job is the satisfaction I receive at the end of each process whenever I know that I have taken a very stressful experience (for the borrowers) and hopefully minimized (if not completely eliminated) all the stress from the experience.

Q. What do you like most and least about your job?

A. It's difficult to say what I like the most about my job as a mortgage broker. As I mentioned earlier, I really get a whole lot of satisfaction out of making this as stress-free a process as possible for people. Most people get very worried thinking about a new mortgage. If I am able to educate them and help them get through the process and understand it a lot better, then I know that I am doing my job correctly. Another thing I really like about my job is that I am self-employed. I can work the hours that I want, the days that I want. And it is very nice having an extremely flexible schedule because it forces you to manage your time extremely wisely. This also ties into one of the things that I like least about my job—working on full commission. So when I close a lot of loans, it's great because I am making a lot of money. But if I go one month closing ZERO loans, I do not get paid. And that can make for some very scary times. Hopefully, those days are over.

Q. What are the three most important professional qualities for mortgage brokers?

A. Punctuality. This is a huge quality in this industry, and the biggest complaint I ever hear about other people in my line of work is that they do not return phone calls in a timely manner, if at all.

Continuing education. There is a lot of competition from other brokers as well as all the other banks competing against one another. It's important that you always keep up with different loan programs and specials because you want to be able to offer products/services that differentiate you from your competition.

Integrity. Referrals, referrals, referrals. That's the name of the game in this business. And if you are not honest and forthcoming with all transactions and all those involved, you are not going to get the valued referrals that you need to grow and sustain your business.

Inspectors

OVERVIEW

Inspectors work for federal, state, and local governments. Their job is to examine the construction, alteration, or repair of buildings and other structures, highways, streets, sewer and water systems, dams, and bridges to ensure that they comply with building codes and ordinances, zoning regulations, and contract specifications. Approximately 84,000 construction and building inspectors are employed in the United States.

HISTORY

Construction is one of the major industries of the modern world. Public construction includes structures such as public housing projects, schools, hospitals, administrative and service buildings, industrial and military facilities, highways, and sewer and water systems.

To ensure the public safety of these structures and systems, various governing bodies establish building codes that contractors must follow. It is the job of the inspector to ensure that the codes are properly followed.

THE JOB

This occupation is made up of four broad categories of specialization: building, electrical, mechanical, and public works.

Building inspectors examine the structural quality of buildings. They check the plans before construction, visit the work site a number of times during construction, and make a final inspection when the project is completed. Some building inspectors specialize in areas such as structural steel or reinforced concrete buildings.

Electrical inspectors visit work sites to inspect the installation of electrical systems and equipment. They check wiring, lighting, generators, and sound and security systems. They may also inspect the wiring for elevators, heating and air-conditioning systems, kitchen appliances, and other electrical installations.

Mechanical inspectors inspect plumbing systems and the mechanical components of heating and air-conditioning equipment and kitchen appliances. They also examine gas tanks, piping, and gas-fired appliances. Some mechanical inspectors specialize in elevators, plumbing, or boilers.

Elevator inspectors inspect both the mechanical and the electrical features of lifting and conveying devices, such as elevators, escalators, and moving sidewalks. They also test their speed, load allowances, brakes, and safety devices.

Plumbing inspectors inspect plumbing installations, water supply systems, drainage and sewer systems, water heater installations, fire sprinkler systems, and air and gas piping systems; they also examine building sites for soil type to determine water table level, seepage rate, and similar conditions.

Heating and refrigeration inspectors examine heating, ventilating, air-conditioning, and refrigeration installations in new buildings and approve alteration plans for those elements in existing buildings.

Home inspectors inspect and report on the condition of a residential property's major systems, components, and structure before their clients sign a sales contract to purchase the property.

Public works inspectors make sure that government construction of water and sewer systems, highways, streets, bridges, and dams conforms to contract specifications. They visit work sites to inspect excavations, mixing and pouring of concrete, and asphalt paving. They also keep records of the amount of work performed and the materials used so that proper payment can be made. These inspectors may specialize in highways, reinforced concrete, or ditches.

Inspectors use measuring devices and other test equipment, take photographs, keep a daily log of their work, and write reports. If any detail of a project does not comply with the various codes, ordinances, or specifications, or if construction is being done without proper permits, the inspectors have the authority to issue a stop-work order.

REQUIREMENTS

High School

People interested in construction inspection must be high school graduates who have taken courses in drafting, algebra, geometry, and English. Additional shop courses will undoubtedly prove helpful as well.

Postsecondary Training

Employers prefer graduates of an apprenticeship program, community or junior college, or people with at least two years toward an engineering or architectural degree. Required courses include construction technology, blueprint reading, technical math, English, and building inspection.

Most inspectors have several years' experience either as a construction contractor or supervisor, or as a craft or trade worker such as a carpenter, electrician, plumber, or pipefitter. This experience demonstrates knowledge of construction materials and practices, which is necessary in inspections. Inspectors receive most of their training on the job.

Certification or Licensing

Some states require certification or licensing for employment. The following professional associations offer certification or registration programs: the International Code Council, the American Construction Inspectors Association, the International Association of Electrical Inspectors, and the National Association of Certified Home

Home inspectors must have an excellent eye for detail and be in good physical condition in order to be able to work in tight areas. *(Ed Bock, Corbis)*

Inspectors. Some states have cooperative agreements with these associations that allow inspectors to become licensed by completing association-sponsored training programs and examinations.

Other Requirements

Inspectors must be precision-minded, have an eye for detail, and be able to accept responsibility. They must be tenacious and patient as they follow each case from investigation to its conclusion. They also must be able to communicate well with others in order to reach a clear analysis of a situation and be able to report this information to a superior or coworker. Inspectors must be able to write effective reports that convey vast amounts of information and investigative work.

Inspectors are expected to have a valid driver's license, as they must be able to travel to and from the construction sites. They must also pass a civil service exam.

EXPLORING

Field trips to construction sites and interviews with contractors or building trade officials are good ways to gain practical information about what it is like to work in the industry and how best to prepare for it. Summer jobs at a construction site provide an overview of the work involved in a building project. Students may also seek part-time jobs with a general contracting company, with a specialized contractor (such as a plumbing or electrical contractor), or as a carpenter's helper. Jobs in certain supply houses will help students become familiar with construction materials.

EMPLOYERS

Approximately 84,000 construction and building inspectors are employed in the United States. Almost half work for local governments, such as municipal or county building departments. Another 21 percent work for architecture or engineering firms. Inspectors employed at the federal level work for such agencies as the Department of Defense or the departments of Housing and Urban Development, Agriculture, and the Interior.

STARTING OUT

People without postsecondary education usually enter the construction industry as a trainee or apprentice. Graduates of technical schools or colleges of construction and engineering can expect to start work as an engineering aide, drafter, estimator, or assistant engineer. Jobs may be found through school career services offices, employment agencies, and unions or by applying directly to contracting company personnel offices. Application may also be made directly to the employment offices of the federal, state, or local governments.

ADVANCEMENT

The federal, state, and large city governments provide formal training programs for their inspectors to keep them abreast of new building code developments and to broaden their knowledge of construction materials, practices, and inspection techniques. Inspectors for small agencies can upgrade their skills by attending state-conducted training programs or taking college or correspondence courses. An engineering degree is usually required to become a supervisory inspector.

EARNINGS

The U.S. Department of Labor reports the median annual income for construction and building inspectors was $43,940 in 2004. The lowest paid 10 percent of these workers had annual earnings of less than $28,140; the highest paid 10 percent made $68,120 or more. Earnings vary based on the inspector's experience, the type of employer, and the location of the work. Salaries are slightly higher in the West and Northwest than in the South and are considerably higher in large metropolitan areas.

WORK ENVIRONMENT

Inspectors work both indoors and outdoors, dividing their time between their offices and the work sites. Inspection sites are dirty and cluttered with tools, machinery, and debris. Although the work is not considered hazardous, inspectors must climb ladders and stairs and crawl under buildings.

The hours are usually regular, but when there is an accident at a site, the inspector has to remain on the job until reports have been completed. The work is steady year-round, rather than seasonal, as are some other construction occupations. In slow construction periods, the inspectors are kept busy examining the renovation of older buildings.

OUTLOOK

As the concern for public safety continues to rise, the demand for inspectors should grow about as fast as the average through 2012 even if construction activity does not increase. The level of new construction fluctuates with the economy, but maintenance and renovation continue during the downswings, so inspectors are rarely laid off. Applicants who have some college education, are already certified inspectors, or who have experience as carpenters, electricians, or plumbers will have the best opportunities. Inspectors tend to be older, more experienced workers who have worked in other construction occupations for many years.

FOR MORE INFORMATION

Contact the following association for information on membership and useful publications:
American Construction Inspectors Association
12995 6th Street, Suite 69
Yucaipa, CA 92399-2549
Tel: 909-795-3039
Email: office@acia.com
http://www.acia.com

For information on state licensing/certification, educational training, careers, and other resources, contact
American Society of Home Inspectors
932 Lee Street, Suite 101
Des Plaines, IL 60016-6546
Tel: 800-743-2744
http://www.ashi.com

For information on careers in electrical inspection and certification, contact
International Association of Electrical Inspectors
901 Waterfall Way, Suite 602
Richardson, TX 75080-7702
Tel: 972-235-1455
http://www.iaei.org

For information on certification, training, and publications, contact
International Code Council
5203 Leesburg Pike, Suite 600
Falls Church, VA 22041

Tel: 888-422-7233
http://www.iccsafe.org

Visit the NACHI's website to read useful publications and view an inspection photo gallery.
National Association of Certified Home Inspectors (NACHI)
PO Box 987
Valley Forge, PA 19482-0987
Tel: 650-429-2057
http://www.nachi.org/contact.htm

For information on home inspection, contact
National Association of Home Inspectors Inc.
4248 Park Glen Road
Minneapolis, MN, 55416
Tel: 952-928-4641
Email: info@nahi.org
http://www.nahi.org

For information on inspection careers in Canada, contact
Canadian Construction Association
75 Albert Street, Suite 400
Ottawa, ON K1P 5E7 Canada
Tel: 613-236-9455
Email: cca@cca-acc.com
http://www.cca-acc.com

Property and Casualty Insurance Agents and Brokers

QUICK FACTS

School Subjects
Business
Mathematics
Speech

Personal Skills
Communication/ideas
Leadership/management

Work Environment
Primarily indoors
Primarily one location

Minimum Education Level
Some postsecondary training

Salary Range
$23,130 to $42,030 to
$111,040

Certification or Licensing
Voluntary (certification)
Required (licensing)

Outlook
More slowly than the average

DOT
250

GOE
10.02.02

NOC
6231

O*NET-SOC
41-3021.00

OVERVIEW

Property and casualty insurance agents and brokers sell policies that help individuals and companies cover expenses and losses from such disasters as fires, burglaries, traffic accidents, and other emergencies. These salespeople also may be known as *fire, casualty, and marine insurance agents or brokers*. There are approximately 30,000 property and casualty insurance agents and brokers employed in the United States.

HISTORY

The development of the property and casualty insurance industry parallels the history of human economic development. This type of insurance was first established in the maritime field. A single shipwreck could put a ship owner out of business, so it became essential for trade financiers to share this risk. Organized maritime insurance began in the late 17th century at Lloyd's coffeehouse in London, where descriptions of individual ships, their cargoes, and their destinations were posted. Persons willing to share the possible loss, in return for a fee, signed their names below these descriptions indicating what percentage of the financial responsibility they were willing to assume. Those who signed were known as "underwriters," a term still used in the insurance business.

As people became more experienced in this procedure, predictions of loss became more accurate and rates were standardized. To provide protection for larger risks, individuals organized companies. The first marine insurance company in the United States—the Insurance Company of North America—was founded in Philadelphia in 1792 and still does business today.

Other types of insurance developed in response to people's need for protection. Insurance against loss by fire became available after the disastrous lesson of the London Fire of 1666. The first accident insurance policy in the United States was sold in 1863. Burglary insurance—protection against property taken by forced entry—was offered soon thereafter. Theft insurance, which covers any form of stealing, was first written in 1899.

Around the turn of the century, the development of the "horseless carriage" led to the automobile insurance industry. The first automobile policy was sold in 1898. This area of the insurance field grew rapidly. In the mid-1990s premiums written for automobile insurance (including liability and collision and comprehensive policies) totaled more than $102 billion.

Growth of business and industrial organizations required companies to offer protection for employees injured on the job. The first workers' compensation insurance was sold in 1910.

Insurance companies have always been alert to new marketing possibilities. In the past few decades, increasing emphasis has been placed upon "package" policies offering comprehensive coverage. A typical package policy is the homeowner's policy, which, in addition to fire protection for the insured's home and property, also covers losses for liability, medical payments, and additional living expenses. In the mid-1950s, a group of private firms provided the first insurance on the multimillion-dollar reactors used in atomic energy plants.

Over the course of the past decade, costs associated with the property and casualty insurance industry (including underwriting losses) have outstripped the annual rate of inflation. This has generally led to an increase in the premium rates charged to customers. The largest increases have occurred in the automobile insurance sector of the industry. The overall trend reflects some basic changes in American society, including a substantial rise in crime and litigation and the development of expensive new medical technologies. The main challenge of the property and casualty insurance industry in the coming years is to stabilize premium rates to remain competitive with alternative forms of risk financing.

THE JOB

Property and casualty insurance salespeople work as either agents or brokers. An agent serves as an authorized representative of an insurance company. A broker, on the other hand, serves as the representative for the client and has no contracts with insurance companies.

Agents can be *independent agents*, *exclusive agents*, or *direct writers*. Independent agents may represent one or more insurance companies, are paid by commission, are responsible for their own expenses, and own the rights to the policies they sell. Exclusive agents represent only one insurance company, are generally paid by commission, are generally responsible for all of their own expenses, and usually own the rights to the policies that they sell. Direct writers represent only one insurance company, are employees of that company (and therefore are often paid a salary and are not responsible for their own expenses), and do not own the rights to the policies that are owned by the company.

Regardless of the system that is used, salespeople operate in a similar fashion. Each one orders or issues policies, collects premiums, renews and changes existing coverage, and assists clients with reports of losses and claims settlement. Backed by the resources of the companies that they represent, individual agents may issue policies insuring against loss or damage for everything from furs and automobiles to ocean liners and factories.

Agents are authorized to issue a "binder" to provide temporary protection for customers between the time the policy application is signed and the policy is issued by the insurance company. Naturally, the agent must be selective in the risks accepted under a binder. Sometimes a risk will be refused by a company, which might cause the agent to lose goodwill with the customer. Because brokers do not directly represent or have contracts with insurance companies, they cannot issue binders.

Some agents or brokers specialize in one type of insurance such as residential home insurance. All agents or brokers, however, must be aware of the kind of protection required by their clients and the exact coverage offered by each company that they represent.

One of the most significant aspects of the property and casualty agent's work is the variety encountered on the job. An agent's day may begin with an important conference with a group of executives seeking protection for a new industrial plant and its related business activities. Following this meeting, the agent may proceed to the office and spend several hours studying the needs of the customer and drafting an insurance plan. This proposal must be thorough and competitively priced because several other local agents will likely be competing for

Did You Know?

- Approximately 607,000 people were employed in the property and casualty insurance industry in 2004.

- In 2004, the property and casualty insurance industry had income of approximately $423 billion in premiums.

- The top five property and casualty insurance companies (by premiums written) in 2004 were State Farm Mutual Group, Allstate Insurance Co. Group, Farmers Insurance Group, Nationwide Group, and St. Paul Travelers Companies and Affiliates.

- Ninety-five percent of homeowners have insurance. The average homeowners' insurance premium was $593 in 2002.

Sources: U.S. Department of Labor, National Underwriter Insurance Data Services/Highline Data, Insurance Research Council, National Association of Insurance Commissioners

the account. While working at the office, the agent usually receives several calls and visits from prospective or current clients asking questions about protection, policy conditions, changes, or new developments.

At noon, the agent may attend a meeting of a service club or have lunch with a policyholder. After lunch, the agent may visit a customer's home to discuss the repairs needed as the result of a downed tree hitting the client's garage. Back at the office, the agent may talk on the telephone with an adjuster from the insurance company involved.

In the late afternoon, the agent may call on the superintendent of schools to discuss insurance protection for a new middle school that is being constructed. The agent evaluates the insurance needs and drafts a proposed policy.

Upon returning to the office, the agent may telephone several customers, dictate responses to the day's mail, and handle other matters that have developed during the day. In the evening, the agent may call on a family to discuss insurance protection for a new home.

REQUIREMENTS
High School
Insurance companies typically insist that their agents have at least a high school diploma, and most strongly prefer their agents to have a college education. There are a number of classes you can take in high school to prepare yourself both for college and for working in the insurance industry. If your high school offers business, economics, or

finance classes, be sure to take advantage of these courses. Mathematics classes will also give you the opportunity to develop your skills working with numbers, which is an important aspect of insurance work. Computer courses will allow you to become familiar with this technology, which you will use throughout your career. In order to develop your communication skills—essential for any salesperson—take English and speech classes. Finally, consider taking classes that will give you insight into people's actions, which is another important skill for a salesperson. Psychology and sociology classes are courses that may offer this opportunity.

Postsecondary Training
Although college training is not a prerequisite for insurance work, those who have a college degree in economics or business will probably have an advantage starting out in this field. Many colleges and universities offer courses in insurance, and a number of schools offer a bachelor's degree in insurance. Classes you are likely to take in college include finance, accounting, and economics. Business law and business administration classes will give you an understanding of legal issues and insurance needs. Also, psychology courses may help you to increase your understanding of people. Finally, keep up with your computer work. Courses that teach you to use software, such as spreadsheet programs, will keep your skills up-to-date and make you more marketable. For some specialized areas of property insurance, such as fire protection for commercial establishments, an engineering background may prove helpful.

Certification or Licensing
Those agents who wish to seek the highest professional status may pursue the designation of chartered property casualty underwriter (CPCU). To earn the designation, agents must complete at least three years in the field successfully, demonstrate high ethical practices in all work, and pass a series of examinations offered by the American Institute for Chartered Property and Casualty Underwriters (AICPCU). Agents and brokers may prepare for these examinations through home study or by taking courses offered by colleges, insurance associations, or individual companies. In 2003, AICPCU introduced a new eight-exam CPCU program that allows agents to specialize in either personal or commercial insurance.

All agents and brokers must obtain licenses from the states in which they sell insurance. Most states require that the agent pass a written examination dealing with state insurance laws and the fundamentals of property and casualty insurance. Often, candidates for licenses must show evidence of some formal study in the field of insurance.

Other Requirements

An agent or broker must thoroughly understand insurance fundamentals and recognize the differences between the many options provided by various policies. This knowledge is essential to gain the respect and confidence of clients. To provide greater service to customers and increase sales volume, beginning agents must study many areas of insurance protection. This requires an analytical mind and the capacity for hard work.

Successful agents and brokers are able to interact with strangers easily and talk readily with a wide range of people. They must be resourceful, self-confident, conscientious, and cheerful. As in other types of sales occupations, a strong belief in the service being sold helps agents to be more successful in their presentations.

Because they spend so much of their time with others, agents and brokers must have a genuine liking for people. Equally important is the desire to serve others by providing financial security. To be successful, they must be able to present insurance information in a clear, nontechnical fashion. They must be able to develop a logical sales sequence and presentation style that is comfortable for prospects and clients.

Successful agents and brokers may participate in community and service activities to stay visible within their communities and to maintain or increase their volume of business. Agents and brokers often have an unusual facility for recalling people's names and past conversations they've had with them.

EXPLORING

Because of state licensing requirements, it is difficult for young people to obtain part-time experience in this field. Summer employment of any sort in an insurance office may give you helpful insights into the field. Because many offices are small and must have someone on premises during business hours, you may find summer positions with individual agencies or brokerage firms. Colleges with work-study programs may offer opportunities for practical experience in an insurance agency.

EMPLOYERS

Approximately 30,000 property and casualty insurance agents and brokers are employed in the United States. Insurance companies are the principal employers; however, some agents and brokers (approximately 25 percent of all insurance salespeople) are self-employed.

STARTING OUT

College graduates are frequently hired through campus interviews for salaried sales positions with major companies. Other graduates secure positions directly with local agencies or brokerages through placement services, employment offices, or classified advertisements in newspapers. Many high school and college graduates apply directly to insurance companies. Sometimes individuals employed in other fields take evening or home-study courses in insurance to prepare for employment in this field.

Once hired, the new agent or broker uses training materials prepared by the company or by industry trade groups. In smaller agencies, newcomers may be expected to assume most of the responsibility for their own training by using the agency's written resources and working directly with experienced agents. In larger organizations, initial training may include formal classroom instruction and enrollment in education programs such as those offered by the American Institute for Chartered Property and Casualty Underwriters. Sometimes insurance societies sponsor courses designed to help the beginning agent. Almost all agents receive directed, on-the-job sales supervision.

ADVANCEMENT

Sales agents may advance in one of several ways. They may decide to establish their own agency or brokerage firm, join or buy out an established agency, or advance into branch or home office management with an insurance company.

Self-employed agents or brokers often remain with the organization that they have developed for the length of their careers. They may grow professionally by expanding the scope of their insurance activities. Many agents expand their responsibilities and their office's sales volume by hiring additional salespeople. Occasionally an established agent may enter related areas of activity. Many property insurance agents, for example, branch out into real estate sales. Many agents and brokers devote an increasing amount of their time to worthwhile community projects, which helps to build goodwill and probable future clients.

EARNINGS

Recently hired sales agents are usually paid a moderate salary while learning the business. After becoming established, however, most agents are paid on the basis of a commission on sales. Agents who work directly for an insurance company often receive a base salary in addition to some commission on sales production. Unlike life insurance agents, who receive a high first-year commission, the property and casualty agent usually receives the same percentage each time the premium is paid.

In 2004, all insurance sales agents (including property and casualty) earned a median salary of $42,030 a year, according to the U.S. Department of Labor. The lowest 10 percent earned $23,130, and the highest 10 percent earned $111,040 or more.

Salespeople employed by companies often receive fringe benefits (such as retirement income, sick leave, and paid vacations), whereas self-employed agents or brokers receive no such benefits.

WORK ENVIRONMENT

Property and casualty insurance agents must be in constant contact with people—clients, prospective clients, and the workers in the home office of the insurance companies. This can be very time-consuming, and occasionally frustrating, but it is an essential element of the work.

Two of the biggest drawbacks to this type of work are the long hours and the irregular schedule. Agents often are required to work their schedules around their clients' availability. Especially in their first years in the business, agents may find that they have to work three or four nights a week and one or two days on the weekend. Most agents work 40 hours a week, but some agents, particularly those just beginning in the field and those with a large clientele, may work 60 hours a week or more.

OUTLOOK

Employment for all insurance agents and brokers is expected to grow more slowly than the average for all occupations through 2012, according to the U.S. Department of Labor. Nevertheless, individuals with determination and the right skills (including fluency in a foreign language, especially Spanish) should have numerous job opportunities for several reasons. The overall demand for insurance should be strong as the general population grows and the amount of personal and corporate possessions increases. Most homeowners and business executives budget insurance as a necessary expense. In addition, laws that require businesses to provide workers' compensation insurance and car owners to obtain automobile liability protection help to maintain an insurance market.

A number of factors, however, are responsible for restraining job growth of insurance agents and brokers. Computers enable agents to perform routine clerical tasks more efficiently, and more policies are being sold by mail and phone. Also, as insurance becomes more and more crucial to their financial health, many large businesses are hiring their own risk managers, who analyze their insurance needs and select the policies that are best for them.

There is a high turnover in this field. Many beginning agents and brokers find it hard to establish a large, profitable client base, and they eventually move on to other areas in the insurance industry. Most openings will occur as a result of this turnover and as workers retire or leave their positions for other reasons.

FOR MORE INFORMATION

For information regarding the CPCU designation, continuing education courses, and industry news, contact
American Institute for Chartered Property and Casualty Underwriters/Insurance Institute of America
720 Providence Road, PO Box 3016
Malvern, PA 19355-0716
Tel: 800-644-2101
Email: cserv@cpcuiia.org
http://www.aicpcu.org

For information on scholarships and women in the insurance industry, contact
Association of Professional Insurance Women
551 Fifth Avenue, Suite 1625
New York, NY 10176
Tel: 212-867-0228
Email: info@apiw.org
http://www.apiw.org

For information on the industry and education programs, contact
Independent Insurance Agents and Brokers of America
127 South Peyton Street
Alexandria, VA 22314
Tel: 800-221-7917
Email: info@iiaba.org
http://www.independentagent.com

For information on educational programs, contact
Insurance Educational Association
100 California Street, Suite 650
San Francisco, CA 94111
Tel: 415-986-6356
Email: info@ieatraining.com
http://www.ieatraining.com

For general information about the insurance industry, contact
Insurance Information Institute
110 William Street
New York, NY 10038
Tel: 212-346-5500
http://www.iii.org

Property and Real Estate Managers

QUICK FACTS

School Subjects
Business
English
Mathematics

Personal Skills
Communication/ideas
Leadership/management

Work Environment
Primarily indoors
Primarily multiple locations

Minimum Education Level
Bachelor's degree

Salary Range
$19,980 to $41,540 to
$91,030

Certification or Licensing
Voluntary (certification)
Required for certain
positions (licensing)

Outlook
About as fast as the average

DOT
186

GOE
13.01.01

NOC
0121

O*NET-SOC
11-9141.00

OVERVIEW

Property and real estate managers plan and supervise the activities that affect land and buildings. Most of them manage rental properties, such as apartment buildings, office buildings, and shopping centers. Others manage the services and commonly owned areas of condominiums and community associations. Approximately 293,000 property and real estate managers are employed in the United States.

HISTORY

The first property managers, in the early 1900s, were real estate agents who earned additional income by collecting rent and negotiating leases. During the 1920s, the job became a menial position that was necessary in a real estate brokerage firm but was not considered a full-fledged part of the business. After the collapse of the financial market in 1929, banks, insurance companies, and other mortgage holders found themselves owners of multiple properties because of foreclosures. These new owners had neither the skills nor the inclination to manage the properties. Suddenly, the position of "rent man," which had been despised in the 1920s, became more respected and more in demand.

The new importance of the property manager, plus a corresponding increase in industry abuses, led to the formation of a professional association for property managers, the Institute of Real Estate Management. The new members quickly set out to establish industry ethics and standards, professional designations, and industry education and seminars.

THE JOB

Most property and real estate managers are responsible for day-to-day management of residential and commercial real estate and usually manage several properties at one time. Acting as the owners' agents and advisers, they supervise the marketing of space, negotiate lease agreements, direct bookkeeping activities, and report to owners on the status of the property. They also negotiate contracts for trash removal and other services and hire the maintenance and on-site management personnel employed at the properties.

Some managers buy and develop real estate for companies that have widespread retail operations, such as franchise restaurants and hotel chains, or for companies that build such projects as shopping malls and industrial parks.

On-site managers are based at the properties they manage and may even live on the property. Most of them are responsible for apartment buildings and work under the direction of property managers. They train, supervise, and assign duties to maintenance staffs; inspect the properties to determine what maintenance and repairs are needed; schedule routine service of heating and air-conditioning systems; keep records of operating costs; and submit cost reports to the property managers or owners. They deal with residents on a daily basis and are responsible for handling their requests for service and repairs, resolving complaints concerning other tenants, and enforcing rules and lease restrictions.

Apartment house managers work for property owners or property management firms and are usually on-site managers. They show apartments to prospective tenants, negotiate leases, collect rents, handle tenants' requests, and direct the activities of maintenance staffs and outside contractors.

Building superintendents are responsible for operating and maintaining the facilities and equipment of such properties as apartment houses and office buildings. At small properties, the superintendent may be the only on-site manager and report directly to property managers; at larger properties, superintendents may report to on-site managers and supervise maintenance staffs.

Housing project managers direct the operation of housing projects provided for such groups as military families, low-income families, and welfare recipients. The housing is usually subsidized by the government and may consist of single-family homes, multiunit dwellings, or house trailers.

Condominium managers are responsible to unit-owner associations and manage the services and commonly owned areas of condominium properties. They submit reports to the association members, supervise collection of owner assessments, resolve owners' complaints, and direct the activities of maintenance staffs and outside contractors. In some communities, such as planned unit developments, homeowners belong to associations that employ managers to oversee the homeowners' jointly used properties and facilities.

Real estate asset managers work for institutional owners such as banks and insurance companies. Their responsibilities are larger in scope. Rather than manage day-to-day property operations, asset managers usually have an advisory role regarding the acquisition, rehabilitation, refinancing, and disposition of properties in a particular portfolio, and they may act for the owner in making specific business decisions, such as selecting and supervising site managers, authorizing operating expenditures, reviewing and approving leases, and monitoring local market conditions.

Specialized property and real estate managers perform a variety of other types of functions. *Market managers* direct the activities of municipal, regional, or state markets where wholesale fruit, vegetables, or meat are sold. They rent space to buyers and sellers and direct the supervisors who are responsible for collecting fees, maintaining and cleaning the buildings and grounds, and enforcing sanitation and security rules. *Public events facilities rental managers* negotiate contracts with organizations that wish to lease arenas, auditoriums, stadiums, or other facilities that are used for public events. They solicit new business and renewals of established contracts, maintain schedules to determine the availability of the facilities for bookings, and oversee operation and maintenance activities.

Real estate firm managers direct the activities of the *sales agents* who work for real estate firms. They screen and hire sales agents and conduct training sessions. They confer with agents and clients to resolve such problems as adjusting selling prices and determining who is responsible for repairs and closing costs. *Business opportunity-and-property-investment brokers* buy and sell business enterprises and investment properties on a commission or speculative basis. They investigate such factors as the financial ratings of businesses that are for sale, the desirability of a property's location for various types of businesses, and the condition of investment properties.

Businesses employ real estate managers to find, acquire, and develop the properties they need for their operations and to dispose of proper-

Top Employers for Property and Real Estate Managers

Industry	Employment	Annual Mean Earnings
Activities Related to Real Estate	50,090	$46,120
Lessors of Real Estate	48,130	$43,920
Offices of Real Estate Agents and Brokers	15,440	$50,830
Local Government	6,820	$54,070
Management of Companies and Enterprises	4,730	$73,760

Source: U.S. Department of Labor, 2004

ties they no longer need. Real estate agents often work for companies that operate retail merchandising chains, such as fast food restaurants, gasoline stations, and apparel shops. They locate sites that are desirable for their companies' operations and arrange to purchase or lease them. They also review their companies' holdings to identify properties that are no longer desirable and then negotiate to dispose of them. (*Real estate sales agents* also may be called real estate agents, but they are not involved in property management.) *Land development managers* are responsible for acquiring land for such projects as shopping centers and industrial parks. They negotiate with local governments, property owners, and public interest groups to eliminate obstacles to their companies' developments, and they arrange for architects to draw up plans and construction firms to build the projects.

REQUIREMENTS

High School
High school students interested in this field should enroll in college preparatory programs that include classes in business, mathematics, speech, and English.

Postsecondary Training
Most employers prefer college graduates for property and real estate management positions. They prefer degrees in real estate, business

management, finance, and related fields, but they also consider liberal arts graduates. In some cases, inexperienced college graduates with bachelor's or master's degrees enter the field as assistant property managers.

Many property and real estate managers attend training programs offered by various professional and trade associations. Employers often send their managers to these programs to improve their management skills and expand their knowledge of such subjects as operation and maintenance of building mechanical systems, insurance and risk management, business and real estate law, and accounting and financial concepts. Many managers attend these programs voluntarily to prepare for advancement to positions with more responsibility.

Certification or Licensing
Certification or licensing is not required for most property managers. Managers who have appropriate experience, complete required training programs, and achieve satisfactory scores on written exams, however, can earn certification and such professional designations as certified property manager and accredited residential manager (which are offered by the Institute of Real Estate Management) and real property administrator and facilities management administrator (which are offered by the BOMI Institute). Such designations are usually looked upon favorably by employers as a sign of a person's competence and dedication.

The federal government requires certification for managers of public housing that is subsidized by federal funds. Business opportunity-and-property-investment brokers must hold state licenses, and some states require real estate managers to hold licenses.

Other Requirements
Property and real estate managers must be skilled in both oral and written communications and be adept at dealing with people. They need to be good administrators and negotiators, and those who specialize in land development must be especially resourceful and creative to arrange financing for their projects. Managers for small rental or condominium complexes may be required to have building repair and maintenance skills as well as business management skills.

EXPLORING

If you are interested in property and real estate management, participate in activities that help you develop management skills, such as serving as an officer in an organization or participating in Junior Achievement projects. Part-time or summer jobs in sales or volunteer work that involves contact with the public would be good experience.

You may be able to tour apartment complexes, shopping centers, and other real estate developments and should take advantage of any opportunities to talk with property and real estate managers about their careers.

EMPLOYERS

Approximately 293,000 people in the United States are employed as property and real estate managers. About 40 percent work for real estate agents and brokers, lessors of real estate, or property management firms. Others work for real estate developers, government agencies that manage public buildings, corporations with large property holdings used for their retail operations, real estate investors, and mining and oil companies. Many are self-employed as developers, apartment building owners, property management firm owners, or owners of full-service real estate businesses. Forty-six percent of all property and real estate managers are self-employed.

STARTING OUT

Students who are about to graduate from college can obtain assistance from their career services offices in finding their first job. You can also apply directly to property management firms and check ads in the help wanted sections of local newspapers. Property and real estate managers often begin as on-site managers for small apartment house complexes, condominiums, or community associations. Some property managers begin as real estate agents or in another position in a real estate firm and later move into property management.

ADVANCEMENT

With experience, entry-level property and site managers may transfer to larger properties or they may become assistant property managers, working closely with property managers and acquiring experience in a variety of management tasks. Assistant managers may advance to property manager positions, in which they most likely will be responsible for several properties. As they advance in their careers, property managers may manage larger or more complex operations, specialize in managing specific types of property, or possibly establish their own companies.

To be considered for advancement, property managers must demonstrate the ability to deal effectively with tenants, contractors, and maintenance staff. They must be capable administrators and possess business skills, initiative, good organization, and excellent communication skills.

EARNINGS

Managers of residential and commercial rental real estate are usually compensated by a fee based on the gross rental income of the properties. Managers of condominiums and other homeowner-occupied properties also are usually paid on a fee basis. Site managers and others employed by a management company are typically salaried.

According to the U.S. Department of Labor, annual earnings for all property managers in 2004 ranged from less than $19,980 to $91,030 or more. The median annual average for property managers in 2004 was $41,540.

Property and real estate managers usually receive such benefits as medical and health insurance. On-site apartment building managers may have rent-free apartments, and many managers have the use of company automobiles. In addition, managers involved in land development may receive a small percentage of ownership in their projects.

WORK ENVIRONMENT

Property and real estate managers usually work in offices but may spend much of their time at the properties they manage. On-site apartment building managers often leave their offices to inspect other areas, check maintenance or repair work, or resolve problems reported by tenants.

Many apartment managers must live in the buildings they manage so they can be available in emergencies, and they may be required to show apartments to prospective tenants at night or on weekends. Property and real estate managers may attend evening meetings with property owners, association boards of directors, or civic groups interested in property planned for development. Real estate managers who work for large companies frequently travel to inspect their companies' property holdings or locate properties their companies might acquire.

OUTLOOK

Employment of property and real estate managers is expected to increase about as fast as the average for all occupations through 2012, according to the U.S. Department of Labor. Job openings are expected to occur as older, experienced managers transfer to other occupations or leave the labor force. The best opportunities will be for college graduates with degrees in real estate, business administration, and related fields.

In the next decade, many of the economy's new jobs are expected to be in wholesale and retail trade, finance, insurance, real estate, and other service industries. Growth in these industries will bring a need for more office and retail properties and for people to manage them.

In housing, there will be a greater demand for apartments because of the high cost of owning a home. New home developments also are increasingly organized with community or homeowner associations that require managers. In addition, more owners of commercial and multiunit residential properties are expected to use professional managers to help make their properties more profitable.

FOR MORE INFORMATION

For information on certification, contact
BOMI Institute
1521 Ritchie Highway
Arnold, MD 21012
Tel: 800-235-2664
Email: service@bomi-edu.org
http://www.bomi-edu.org

For information on educational programs, contact
Building Owners and Managers Association International
1201 New York Avenue, NW, Suite 300
Washington, DC 20005
Tel: 202-408-2662
Email: info@boma.org
http://www.boma.org

For information on training programs, certification, and industry research, contact
Institute of Real Estate Management
430 North Michigan Avenue
Chicago, IL 60611

Tel: 800-837-0706
Email: custserv@irem.org
http://www.irem.org

This organization is devoted to the multifamily housing industry and represents developers, owners, managers, and suppliers.
National Apartment Association
201 North Union Street, Suite 200
Alexandria, VA 22314
Tel: 703-518-6141
http://www.naahq.org

For information on property management in Canada, contact
Canadian Real Estate Association
344 Slater Street, Suite 1600
Canada Building
Ottawa, ON K1R 7Y3 Canada
Tel: 613-237-7111
Email: info@crea.ca
http://crea.ca

Real Estate Agents and Brokers

OVERVIEW

Real estate brokers are business people who sell, rent, or manage the property of others. *Real estate agents* are salespeople who are either self-employed or hired by brokers. Sometimes, the term *agent* is applied to both real estate brokers and agents. There are approximately 308,000 real estate agents and 99,000 real estate brokers employed in the United States.

HISTORY

Three factors contributed to the rise of the modern real estate business: first, the general increase in the total population and in the number of pieces of real estate for sale; second, the growing percentage of people owning property; and third, the complexity of laws regarding the transfer of real estate. These factors led to the need for experienced agents, on whom both sellers and buyers increasingly rely.

Professionalization of the real estate field developed rapidly in the 20th century. In 1908, the National Association of Realtors was founded. This huge trade group has encouraged the highest ethical standards for the field and has lobbied hard in Congress for many of the tax advantages that homeowners and property owners now enjoy.

QUICK FACTS

School Subjects
Business
English
Mathematics

Personal Skills
Communication/ideas
Helping/teaching

Work Environment
Primarily indoors
Primarily multiple locations

Minimum Education Level
High school diploma

Salary Range
$18,570 to $36,950 to
$101,310+

Certification or Licensing
Required

Outlook
More slowly than the average

DOT
250

GOE
10.03.01

NOC
6232

O*NET-SOC
41-9021.00, 41-9022.00

THE JOB

The primary responsibility of real estate brokers and agents is to help clients buy, sell, rent, or lease a piece of real estate. Real estate is a piece of land or property and all improvements attached to it. The property may be residential, commercial, or agricultural. When people wish to put property up for sale or rent, they contract with real estate brokers to arrange the sale and to represent them in the transaction. This contract with a broker is called a listing.

One of the main duties of brokers is to actively solicit listings for the agency. They develop leads for potential listings by distributing promotional items, by advertising in local publications, and by showing other available properties in open houses. They also spend a great deal of time on the phone exploring leads gathered from various sources, including personal contacts.

Once a listing is obtained, real estate agents analyze the property to best present it to prospective buyers. They have to recognize and promote the property's strong selling points. A *residential real estate agent* might emphasize such attributes as a home's layout or proximity to schools, for example. Agents develop descriptions to be used with photographs of the property in ads and promotions. To make a piece of real estate more attractive to prospective buyers, agents may also advise homeowners on ways to improve the look of their property to be sold.

Agents are also responsible for determining the fair market value for each property up for sale. They compare their client's real estate with similar properties in the area that have recently been sold to decide upon a fair asking price. The broker and any agents of the brokerage work to obtain the highest bid for a property because their earnings are dependent on the sale price. Owners usually sign a contract agreeing that if their property is sold, they will pay the agent a percentage of the selling price.

When the property is ready to be shown for sale, agents contact buyers and arrange a convenient time for them to see the property. If the property is vacant, the broker usually retains the key. To adjust to the schedules of potential buyers, agents frequently show properties in the late afternoon or evening and on weekends. Because a representative of the broker's firm is usually on the premises in each house, weekend showings are a good way to put part-time or beginning agents to work.

An agent may have to meet several times with a prospective buyer to discuss and view available properties. When the buyer decides on a property, the agent must bring the buyer and seller together at terms agreeable to both. In many cases, different brokers will represent the seller and buyer. Agents may have to present several counteroffers to reach a compromise suitable to both parties.

A real estate agent goes over paperwork with a young couple who are about to purchase their first home. *(Diaphor Agency/Index Stock Imagery)*

Once the contract is signed by both the buyer and the seller, the agent must see to it that all terms of the contract are carried out before the closing date. For example, if the seller has agreed to repairs or a home inspection, the agent must make sure it is carried out or the sale cannot be completed.

Brokers often provide buyers with information on loans to finance their purchase. They also arrange for title searches and title insurance. A broker's knowledge, resourcefulness, and creativity in arranging financing that is favorable to the buyer can mean the difference between success and failure in closing a sale. In some cases, agents assume the responsibilities of closing the sale, but this is increasingly handled by lawyers or loan officers.

Commercial or agricultural real estate agents operate in much the same fashion. Their clients usually have specific and prioritized needs. For example, a trucking firm might require their property to be located near major highways. These real estate specialists often conduct extensive searches to meet clients' specifications. They usually make fewer but larger sales resulting in higher commissions.

In addition to selling real estate, some brokers rent and manage properties for a fee. Some brokers combine other types of work, such as selling insurance or practicing law, with their real estate businesses.

REQUIREMENTS

High School
There are no standard educational requirements for the real estate field. However, high school courses in English, business, and math would help to prepare you for communicating with clients and handling sales.

Postsecondary Training
An increasing percentage of real estate agents and brokers have some college education. As property transactions have become more complex, many employers favor applicants with more education. Courses in psychology, economics, sociology, marketing, finance, business administration, and law are helpful. Many colleges also offer specific courses or even degrees in real estate.

Certification or Licensing
Every state (and the District of Columbia) requires that real estate agents and brokers be licensed. For the general license, most states require agents to be at least 18 years old, have between 30 and 90 hours of classroom training, and pass a written examination on real estate fundamentals and state laws. Prospective brokers must pass a more extensive examination and complete between 60 and 90 hours of classroom training. Additionally, many states require brokers to have prior experience selling property or a formal degree in real estate.

State licenses are usually renewed annually without examination, but many states require agents to fulfill continuing education requirements in real estate. Agents who move to another state must qualify under the licensing laws of that state. To supplement minimum state requirements, many agents take courses in real estate principles, laws, financing, appraisal, and property development and management.

Other Requirements
Successful brokers and agents must be willing to study the changing trends of the industry to keep their skills updated. Residential real estate agents must keep up with the latest trends in mortgage financing, construction, and community development. They must have a thorough knowledge of the housing market in their assigned communities so they can identify which neighborhoods will best fit their clients' needs and budgets, and they must be familiar with local zoning and tax laws. Agents and brokers must also be good negotiators to act as go-betweens between buyers and sellers.

In most cases, educational experience is less important than the right personality. Brokers want agents who possess a pleasant personality, exude honesty, and maintain a neat appearance. Agents must work with many different types of people and inspire their trust and confidence. They need to express themselves well and show enthusiasm to motivate customers. They should also be well organized and detail oriented, as well as have a good memory for names, faces, and business details.

EXPLORING

Contact local real estate brokers and agents for useful information on the field and to talk one-on-one with an employee about their job. You can also obtain information on licensing requirements from local real estate boards or from the real estate departments of each state. Securing part-time and summer employment in a real estate office will provide you with practical experience.

EMPLOYERS

There are approximately 407,000 real estate agents and brokers currently employed in the United States. Many work part time, supplementing their income with additional jobs in law, finance, or other fields.

Agents work in small offices, larger organizations, or for themselves. (Six out of ten real estate agents and brokers are self-employed.) Opportunities exist at all levels, from large real estate firms specializing in commercial real estate to smaller, local offices that sell residential properties. Much of agents' work is independent; over time, they can develop their own client bases and set their own schedules.

STARTING OUT

The typical entry position in this field is as an agent working for a broker with an established office. Another opportunity may be through inside sales, such as with a construction firm building new housing developments. Prospective agents usually apply directly to local real estate firms or are referred through public and private employment services. Brokers looking to hire agents may run newspaper advertisements. Starting out, prospective agents often contact firms in their own communities, where their knowledge of the neighborhood can work to their advantage.

The beginning agent must choose between the advantages of joining a small or a large organization. In a small office, the newcomer will train informally under an experienced agent. Their duties will be broad and varied but possibly menial. However, this is a good chance to learn all the basics of the business, including gaining familiarity with the computers used to locate properties or sources of financing. In larger firms, the new agent often proceeds through a more standardized training process and specializes in one phase of the real estate field, such as commercial real estate, mortgage financing, or property management.

ADVANCEMENT

While many successful agents develop professionally by expanding the quality and quantity of their services, others seek advancement by entering management or by specializing in residential or commercial real estate. An agent may enter management by becoming the head of a division of a large real estate firm. Other agents purchase an established real estate business, join one as a partner, or set up their own offices. Self-employed agents must meet state requirements and obtain a broker's license.

Agents who wish to specialize have a number of available options. They may develop a property management business. In return for approximately 5 percent of the gross receipts, *property managers* operate apartment houses or multiple-tenant business properties for their owners. Property managers are in charge of renting (including advertising, tenant relations, and collecting rents), building maintenance (heating, lighting, cleaning, and decorating), and accounting (financial recording and filing tax returns).

Agents can also become *appraisers,* estimating the current market value of land and buildings, or *real estate counselors,* advising clients on the suitability of available property. Experienced brokers can also join the real estate departments of major corporations or large government agencies.

EARNINGS

Compensation in the real estate field is based largely upon commission. Agents usually split commissions with the brokers who employ them, in return for providing the office space, advertising support, sales supervision, and the use of the broker's good name. When two or more agents are involved in a transaction (for example, one agent listing the property for sale and another selling it), the commission is usually divided between the two on the basis of an established formula. Agents can earn more if they both list and sell the property.

According to the U.S. Department of Labor, median annual earnings of salaried real estate agents, including commission, were $36,950 in 2004. Salaries ranged from less than $18,570 to more than $101,310. Median annual earnings of salaried real estate brokers, including commission, were $56,970 in 2004, and salaries ranged from less than $23,260 to more than $95,210 a year.

Agents and brokers may supplement their incomes by appraising property, placing mortgages with private lenders, or selling insurance. Since earnings are irregular and economic conditions unpredictable, agents and brokers should maintain sufficient cash reserves for slack periods.

WORK ENVIRONMENT

One glance at the property advertisements in any newspaper will offer a picture of the high competition found within the field of real estate. In addition to full-time workers, the existence of many part-time agents increases competition.

Beginning agents must accept the frustration inherent in the early months in the business. Earnings are often irregular before a new agent has built a client base and developed the skills needed to land sales.

After agents become established, many work more than 40 hours a week, including evenings and weekends. Despite this, agents work on their own schedules and are free to take a day off when they choose. Some do much of their work out of their own homes. However, successful agents will spend little time in an office; they are busy showing properties to potential buyers or meeting with sellers to set up a listing.

Real estate positions are found in every part of the country but are concentrated in large urban areas and in smaller, rapidly growing communities. Regardless of the size of the community in which they work, good agents should know its economic life, the personal preferences of its citizens, and the demand for real estate.

OUTLOOK

According to the *Occupational Outlook Handbook,* employment of agents and brokers is expected to grow more slowly than the average for all occupations through 2012. Turnover within the field is high; new job opportunities surface as agents retire or transfer to other types of work.

The country's expanding population also creates additional demand for real estate services. A trend toward mobility, usually among Americans in their prime working years, indicates a continued need for real estate professionals. In addition, a higher percentage of affluence among this working group indicates that more Americans will be able to own their own homes.

An increase in agents' use of technology, such as computers, faxes, and databases, has greatly improved productivity. Computer-generated images now allow agents and customers to view multiple property listings without leaving the office. However, the use of this technology may eliminate marginal jobs, such as part-time workers, who may not be able to invest in this technology and compete with full-time agents.

The field of real estate is easily affected by changes in the economy. Periods of prosperity bring a lot of business. Conversely, a downturn leads to a lower number of real estate transactions, resulting in fewer sales and commissions for agents and brokers.

FOR MORE INFORMATION

For information on licensing, contact
Association of Real Estate License Law Officials
PO Box 230159
Montgomery, AL 36123-0159
Tel: 334-260-2902
Email: mailbox@arello.org
http://www.arello.org

For information on commercial real estate, contact
Society of Industrial and Office Realtors
1201 New York Avenue, NW, Suite 350
Washington, DC 20005-6126
Tel: 202-449-8200
Email: admin@sior.com
http://www.sior.com

For information on state and local associations, professional designations, real estate courses, and publications, contact
National Association of Realtors
430 North Michigan Avenue
Chicago, IL 60611
Tel: 312-329-8292
http://www.realtor.org

Real Estate Developers

OVERVIEW

Real estate developers envision, organize, and execute construction or renovation projects for commercial or private use. This process involves negotiation with property owners, real estate agents, investors, lending institutions such as banks and insurance companies, architects, lawyers, general contractors, government officials, and other interested parties. Developers may work independently as consultants or in partnership with other professionals involved in real estate development.

HISTORY

The United States is a relatively young country without a long history of densely populated cities. In Europe, however, there is evidence of city-dwelling patterns from as far back as 3,000 years ago. In areas of early Roman settlement, archaeologists have discovered the remnants of street grids, sewage lines, and uniform construction indicating some level of formal planning. Since the Middle Ages, Paris has had municipal regulations governing the placement and use of buildings.

Such planning and regulations emerge when many people try to live harmoniously in a limited space. In these situations, land has value and, therefore, it is expensive. Construction of homes, roads for travel, or public buildings for commerce and government requires a substantial investment of money. The developer is the entrepreneur who sees an opportunity to make money by providing services, in the form of buildings or infrastructure, to the community. The developer's role throughout history has been to envision development, organize investors to fund land purchase and construction, and oversee the project.

Individuals have played this role in much the same way as long as people have lived in settled communities. What has changed, and what continues to change, are the zoning laws and building codes regulating development and the tax laws affecting the organization of the development entity.

THE JOB

A developer may be involved in purchasing 500 suburban acres and developing 1,000 condominiums, a couple of parks, a golf course, and a small shopping center with a grocery store, full-service dry cleaner, video rental store, and health club. Or a developer may renovate and remodel an existing structure, such as a warehouse, for use as a restaurant and office space. The developer's actual day-to-day activities vary depending on the type and size of the project.

Whether a group of investors approaches the developer or the developer searches out investors, the first step is to structure the *development entity,* a group made up of the *project owner* (the person or group who will receive the profits or suffer the losses from the proposed development), the *investors* who put up the initial equity funds, and the developer. In many cases, the developer is the owner. These individuals may establish a development entity with only one owner, a partnership with a lead owner, a limited partnership, or a corporation that sells stock to stockholders.

The legal definitions of each type of entity vary according to locale, and the benefits and risks of each are quite different. The developer, who facilitates the process of structuring the contract, is concerned with three main issues—managing risk, gathering equity to facilitate borrowing money, and creating a functioning structure with a limited number of people involved in decision-making.

The developer's job at the beginning of a project has been compared to pitching a tent in high wind. The toughest thing is getting the first corner nailed down. In negotiating with potential investors, the developer brings all interested parties to the table to secure an initial commitment of equity funds. Without equity, the developer is unable to approach banks or insurance companies for loans to complete the project.

The developer may come to the table with $100,000 of personal money to invest—or none. With an excellent track record and a solid proposal, the developer's involvement in the project may be enough to secure the confidence of potential investors. But the developer must show a willingness to protect these investors by creating a development entity that exposes them only to reasonable risk.

Most investors want to risk only the equity money they contribute. In other words, if the project fails, they do not want to be held liable for all the money lost. The contract needs to protect their other assets, such as their homes, savings accounts, and other investments, in case of a default on the loans. So the contract must be written in such a way that the investors are willing to accept the risk involved.

After securing the equity necessary to convince financial institutions to participate in the project, the developer approaches these institutions (primarily banks and insurance companies) to secure financing.

Most development projects require both short-term and long-term financing. Banks often provide the money to buy land and complete construction. However, to receive this short-term financing, sometimes called a *construction loan,* the developer must already have equity funds from the investors. The equity money might equal from 10 to 40 percent of the total amount of the loan.

Insurance companies are the most common providers of long-term financing, which is used to pay off the construction loan. Long-term financing commitments are based on the economic projections of the completed development and usually must be obtained before securing short-term financing. Occasionally one institution will provide both the short-term and long-term financing, but this is less likely to happen with larger projects.

Another participant in real estate financing is the government. Sometimes a municipal government will issue a bond to raise money from taxes. These funds may provide long-term financing to a private developer for the construction of a stadium, for example, or for some infrastructure improvement, such as widening the streets. Municipal governments frequently participate in projects to develop run-down areas of the city. In exchange for shouldering some of the financial risk, the city stands to benefit from the increased productivity of the renovated neighborhood.

Before receiving a building permit, the real estate developer may have to complete impact studies to assess how the proposed project will affect the community and the environment. He or she may also have to meet with the zoning board if there are regulations that the new building will be unable to meet.

At this stage, the project needs an *architect.* The architect's first job usually is to hire a *structural engineer* and a *mechanical engineer.*

Together they create the building plans, which the developer submits to the building department.

This process of creating the plans involves consideration of economics, aesthetic architectural concerns, environmental concerns, building codes, and other legal constraints imposed by the community. This is one of the most exciting and important times in the development process. Through the competition of the interests of all the involved parties, the best use for the site evolves, and the project is born.

While waiting for the building permit to be issued, the developer also puts the building plans out for bids from *general contractors.* The general contractor selected for the job hires subcontractors, such as carpenters, plumbers, roofers, and drywallers.

In applying for the building permit and preparing to break ground on the construction site, developers spend a lot of time dealing with government regulations. They must make sure that they understand and meet building codes designed to ensure the safety of future occupants. Windows in a residential building, for example, must have a certain number of square feet for light and a certain number for ventilation.

Developers must be aware not only of building codes but also of laws affecting construction. New buildings, for example, must meet handicap access codes to comply with the Americans with Disabilities Act.

On large projects, such as the development of a skyscraper in downtown Chicago, the developer will contract out much of the work, such as public relations and advertising, the completion of impact studies, and the general contractor's job. On smaller projects, however, the developer may perform some or all of these functions.

As general contractor, the developer is involved on a daily basis with work at the construction site. If someone else is hired as general contractor, the developer may be involved only at weekly construction meetings, where the architect, engineers, and various subcontractors discuss progress and changes necessary in the plans.

In either case, the developer, who is ultimately responsible for the success or failure of the project, must be knowledgeable about all aspects of the development process and capable of hiring a group of people who can work successfully as a team. Though the developer may or may not be an investor who stands to lose money, the developer's career is on the line with every project.

If a developer secures city approval and necessary funds to construct a new office building in a highly visible spot, the whole city

Real estate developer
Donald Trump
responds to a question
from a reporter during
a television interview.
*(Emile Wamsteker/
Bloomberg, Landov)*

may be watching. The local government officials may have used their influence to change zoning laws in favor of the project. Therefore, their reputations also may be riding on the building's success. If, for example, the construction costs exceed the initial estimates, and the developer is unable to raise the additional money to cover the costs, construction on the building may be halted at any stage, and the empty shell may stand for years as an eyesore in the community.

Failure to successfully complete such projects inhibits the developer's ability to secure investors and government cooperation in the future. Depending on the terms of the developer's contract, it may also mean that the developer is never compensated for the time and work spent on the project.

Once the project is complete, the developer's role depends on the specifications set forth by the development entity. With a high-rise residential building, for example, the developer may be involved in selling or renting the apartments. As an owner in the project, the developer may be involved in the management of rental property for many years.

REQUIREMENTS
High School
There are no specific educational requirements or certifications for becoming a real estate developer, but many developers have college degrees, and some have advanced degrees. While you are in high school, you can prepare for a career in real estate development by pursuing a broad-based liberal arts curriculum that will prepare you for a college education. In addition, courses in business, economics, finance, mathematics, speech communications, drafting, and shop will be helpful.

Postsecondary Training
Schools generally do not offer a specific curriculum that leads to a career as a real estate developer. Because the position requires a broad base of knowledge as well as some experience in the business community, most people become real estate developers after leaving an earlier career.

There are a few schools that offer undergraduate degrees in real estate, usually as a concentration within a general business degree program. Ohio State University, for example, offers a bachelor's degree in Real Estate and Urban Analysis (http://fisher.osu.edu/programs/undergraduate/academics/specializations). There are even fewer graduate degree programs in real estate, such as the University of South Carolina's master's in real estate development (http://mooreschool.sc.edu/moore/finance/fina-home.htm). (Note: The university also offers an undergraduate major in real estate.) Some schools offer master of business administration programs with a concentration in real estate.

Graduate degrees in law, business, and architecture are among the most beneficial to the real estate developer. If you are interested in pursuing an advanced degree in one of these areas, you should complete the necessary preparatory work as an undergraduate.

To pursue a law degree, you need a strong background in the liberal arts, including English, philosophy, history, and government. Good preparation for a master's degree in business includes course work in finance, marketing, accounting, business communications, and higher-level mathematics. An advanced degree in architecture requires an emphasis on drafting, mathematics, engineering, and physics.

Other Requirements
Real estate development is regarded as one of the most challenging careers in the real estate industry. You must have the ability to

speculate about the economy and envision profitable ventures as well as have a broad knowledge of the legal, financial, political, and construction issues related to development. Consequently, a background in law, architecture, or general contracting can be highly beneficial.

It is useful to have a working knowledge of both zoning laws and building codes. While it is the architect's primary responsibility to ensure that the plans ultimately submitted to the building department will be approved, the knowledgeable developer may decide it is appropriate to seek a variance in zoning or code. This is most common in nonsafety areas, such as the number of parking spaces required. A municipality might grant a variance if you present a convincing case that the project will create a significant number of jobs for the community.

You also must understand the marketplace. For this reason, experience in appraising, leasing, or selling real estate can prove very helpful. Real estate brokers who lease office space often have excellent contacts and knowledge for entering the development business. They know where the potential tenants are, and they understand the issues involved in developing large buildings for commercial use. You also must grasp the basics of finance to structure the development entity effectively.

EXPLORING

Read the real estate section of your local newspaper and follow the building and development activities in your community to gain exposure to this industry. Your local librarian should also be able to refer you to books and magazines about real estate development. Sometimes a teacher will be able to arrange for a developer or other real estate professional to visit and talk about his or her work.

You can also prepare for your careers by working in the offices of the following professionals: real estate developers, lawyers practicing within the real estate industry, architects, and general contractors. Spending time in any of these offices will introduce you to the general milieu of the real estate developer's world. The early exposure can also help you decide in which of these areas you most want to develop expertise.

You can gain good experience in certain aspects of real estate development by doing public relations, publicity, or advertising work and participating in fund-raising campaigns for school and community organizations. Volunteering with a housing advocacy organization, such as Habitat for Humanity, may provide opportunities to learn about home construction, bank financing, and legal contracts. To gain confidence and develop a business sense, take on leadership roles at school and in extracurricular activities, such as the student council or the business club.

EMPLOYERS

Real estate developers often work independently or open offices in communities that have property with the potential for development. The activity of the real estate marketplace will dictate the number of opportunities in a given community.

STARTING OUT

There is no specific way to become a real estate developer. Successful real estate developers are always the heart of the project, facilitating communication among the various participants. This often requires finely tuned diplomatic skills. Their proven track record, professional manner, and influence in the real estate world are their biggest assets. They have the ability to sell ideas and secure large sums of money from investors and lending institutions.

Most developers do not begin their careers in this field. They frequently have backgrounds as lawyers, architects, real estate brokers, or general contractors, positions that allow them to gain the expertise and contacts necessary for success in real estate development.

Many real estate developers secure work because they have an established reputation. Their contacts and knowledge in a particular community or type of real estate allow them to work more effectively than others. But developers also are successful because of their abilities in analyzing the marketplace, structuring solid investment proposals, facilitating the creation of the development entity, and overseeing projects.

ADVANCEMENT

The real estate developer is really at the top of the profession. Advancement involves larger, more prestigious projects and earning more money. Such achievement may take several years. It is important to keep in mind that even the most successful developers suffer setbacks when projects fail. For those not-so-successful developers, such setbacks can end a career.

EARNINGS

There is no set pay scale for real estate developers. How much they make depends on their skill and experience, the size of the projects they work on, the structure established for their payment in the development entity contract, and the successful completion of the project.

Sometimes, developers are contracted by a group of individual investors or a company to manage a project. In this case they may work out a consulting agreement with a certain secured fee up front, preset fees paid throughout the duration of the project, and some percentage of the profits once the project is complete. Or the agreement may contain some combination of these payment options.

A less experienced developer will often shoulder more risk on a project to gain expertise and complete work that will improve the developer's reputation. In these instances, developers may be undercompensated or not paid at all for their time and effort if the project fails.

According to the Ford Career Center of the University of Texas, graduates with a bachelor's degree in business administration working in real estate earned an average salary of $42,467 in 2005. The average salary for MBA graduates in real estate was $75,058. Experienced developers can make well over $100,000 year.

WORK ENVIRONMENT

Real estate developers are often highly visible individuals in the community. It is important that they have excellent communication skills, be able to work with all kinds of people, and enjoy the speculative nature of the business.

Developers spend a great deal of time negotiating with executives in banks and insurance companies, government officials, and private or corporate business investors. A certain professionalism and comfort in executive situations is necessary for success.

However, some developers report to the job site every day, don a hard hat, and oversee the work of roofers, plumbers, and electricians. The developer must be flexible enough to adjust to the job's varying demands.

In addition to staying in touch with investors and overseeing the project, developers sometimes may need to respond to the public and the media. Controversial, high-profile projects often put the developer under a spotlight, requiring excellent public relations skills.

Real estate developers, because of the complexity of their jobs and the often large sums of money at stake, work under a great deal of pressure and stress. While the level of risk and the potential profit depend on the developer's role in the development entity, those who like a steady schedule with a dependable paycheck may not be well-suited to this career.

Hours can be long and frequently vary with the type of project and stage of development. Developers may have to attend city council meetings or neighborhood meetings in the evening if they are seeking changes in zoning laws before applying for a building permit. In addition to having the potential to earn a large sum of money, developers enjoy the satisfaction of seeing a project evolve from idea inception through various stages of planning and finally into a finished usable structure.

Though their work depends on the cooperation of other individuals and organizations, developers also enjoy a certain level of independence and flexibility in their lifestyles. As entrepreneurs, they shoulder a lot of personal risk for their businesses, but this brings with it great opportunities to do creative work and positively influence their communities while potentially earning a handsome profit.

OUTLOOK

The outlook for real estate developers is subject to the fluctuations of the general economy. Record-low interest rates have created strong employment opportunities for real estate professionals, but economic conditions are never fixed. In addition, the real estate market can be quite strong in some parts of the country and weak in others. Real estate developers who stay up-to-date with current trends in the industry will have the best employment prospects.

FOR MORE INFORMATION

For information on the real estate industry and career opportunities, contact
National Association of Realtors
430 North Michigan Avenue
Chicago, IL 60611
Tel: 312-329-8292
http://www.realtor.com

For information on real estate lenders and other related topics, contact
The Real Estate Library
http://www.relibrary.com

INTERVIEW

Julie Norris is the vice president of operations at McHugh Development & Construction Inc. in Chicago, Illinois. She has been a real estate developer for almost 10 years, specializing in high-end single-family homes, town homes, and condominiums. Julie discussed her career with the editors of Careers in Focus: Real Estate.

Q. What are your typical responsibilities as a real estate developer?

A. My responsibilities include contract negotiations, design and site planning, zoning and environmental planning, and sales and marketing. Every day offers something new and interesting. I can start the morning meeting with my architects and designers to lay out the interior of a home and end the day wearing boots and a hard hat at a site reviewing foundation stakes. You must be able to wear many hats and be able to change gears quickly in this profession. Decisions that affect your project are required daily, and you need to be able to make those decisions quickly and efficiently and move on to the next task.

Q. What advice would you give to high school students who are interested in this career?

A. Real estate development is a great career if you like a fast-paced environment. Finding properties and making deals is like looking for treasures. It takes time and patience, but the end result is exciting.

Q. What are the three most important professional qualities for real estate developers?

A. 1. Communication is key. In real estate development, you need to be able to communicate with attorneys and architects one minute and carpenters and bricklayers the next. The ability to effectively communicate with people from all walks of life is a great challenge.

2. Persistence. Good deals don't fall in your lap. And even when you find a deal, you have to deal with a lot of bureaucracy to get your projects up and running. If one strategy isn't working, you need to switch strategies and try another route. You need to be able to break through the barriers or find a path around them to get your projects completed.

3. Salesmanship and confidence. You are constantly selling yourself and your product. Everyone you meet is a potential

buyer. You have to speak up and tell people who you are and what you have accomplished. If you make a great product, be proud and tell the world.

Q. What do you like least and most about your job?

A. I dislike dealing with uncooperative subcontractors and bureaucracy. These are a constant challenge, but with patience and persistence, you can be successful.

I love building homes. And I love seeing the end result of hard work—happy homeowners. There is great satisfaction knowing that you had a hand in creating the place where families come together and create lifelong memories.

Real Estate Educators

OVERVIEW

Real estate educators, or *real estate teachers,* provide postsecondary instruction to students wishing to enter the real estate industry. They also offer continuing education opportunities or training to those already committed to a real estate career. They teach in colleges and universities, as well as in smaller classroom settings such as park districts, for-profit proprietary schools, conferences, and real estate corporations. Many belong to the Real Estate Educators Association, which serves the interests of real estate teachers nationwide.

HISTORY

In American colonial times, organized adult education was started to help people make up for schooling missed as children or to help people prepare for jobs. Apprenticeships were an early form of vocational education in the American colonies as individuals were taught a craft by working with a skilled person in a particular field.

Peak periods in adult education typically occurred during times of large-scale immigration. Evening schools filled with foreign-born persons eager to learn the language and culture of their new home and to prepare for the tests necessary for citizenship.

In 1911, Wisconsin established the first State Board of Vocational and Adult Education in the country, and in 1917 the federal government supported the continuing education movement by funding vocational training in public schools for individuals over the age of 14. Immediately after World War II, the federal government took another large stride in financial support of adult and vocational education by creating the G.I. Bill of Rights, which provided money for veterans to pursue further job training.

Today, colleges and universities, vocational high schools, private trade schools, private businesses, and other organizations offer adults the opportunity to prepare for a specific occupation or pursue personal enrichment. Real estate, with its many opportunities, is a popular choice. Today, real estate education is available throughout the United States, in different disciplines and venues. Many schools' real estate curriculum is accredited by either the National Association of Realtors or meets licensure requirements as dictated by the state in which the schools are located.

THE JOB

Real estate education classes take place in a variety of settings, such as high schools, colleges and universities, community centers, and businesses. The responsibilities of a real estate teacher are similar to those of a schoolteacher and include planning and conducting lectures, grading homework, evaluating students, writing and preparing reports, and counseling students.

When employed at colleges or universities, real estate educators are referred to as *instructors* or *professors*. They hold an advanced degree in real estate or related field, such as business or law. In addition, many have years of practical real estate experience. This expertise and insight adds greatly to the instruction they provide their students. Students who complete these types of programs graduate with an undergraduate or graduate degree in real estate, or a business degree with a concentration in real estate.

A larger number of real estate educators teach at community colleges, vocational schools, for-profit real estate schools, or park districts. Many, but not all, educators at this level hold a college degree in real estate or business. Others obtain their positions solely on the merit of their career experience. They may teach classes for college credit towards a certificate or associate degree. Others may teach a one-session adult enrichment class or noncredit courses lasting for an entire semester. They may teach classes pertaining to property appraisal standards and ethics, real estate law, mortgage brokering, commercial property management, or countless other topics. Educators at this level may also prepare students for exams needed to obtain a real estate broker's license or property appraiser's license. They may teach certification classes such as those needed to become a home inspector.

Many real estate teachers are also employed by real estate corporations to provide their staff additional education or training. The Real Estate Educator's Association (REAA) estimates that between 5,000 to 6,000 educators are employed throughout the United States to provide agents and brokers information on the latest trends and developments in contract law, mortgage financing and disclosure, and other topics. Others real estate teachers are tapped to provide sales agents additional training to boost job performance.

Well-known and respected professionals in the real estate industry are often contracted by associations or corporations to teach seminars at conferences and training sessions. Their advice, approach, and experience are often inspirational to those still climbing the real estate corporate ladder.

Whether teaching in higher education or a continuing education classroom, real estate teachers, in addition to giving lectures, assign textbook readings and homework assignments. They prepare and administer exams and grade essays and presentations. Real estate teachers also meet with students individually to discuss class progress and grades. Some courses are conducted as part of a long-distance education program (traditionally known as correspondence courses). Many of these classes are now taught online. For these classes, teachers prepare course materials, assignments, and work schedules to be sent to students, and then grade the work when the students turn it in.

REQUIREMENTS

High School
While in high school, you should take college preparatory classes such as business, English, math, history, and government. Speech and communications courses will help you prepare for speaking in front of groups of people. Writing skills are very important because you'll be preparing reports, lesson plans, and grading essays. Take classes such as English and social studies, which often require written reports to help you perfect your research and writing skills. Teachers use computers to do research, write reports, calculate and report grades, as well as to conduct online lessons. Increase your computer comfort level by taking all computer classes your school has to offer.

Postsecondary Training
Before becoming a real estate teacher, you'll need to gain some professional experience in this area. A bachelor's degree is often

required in real estate, business, or a related field, though some colleges and universities will only consider those with a master's degree or higher. Many faculty members teaching at top tier conferences hold advanced degrees in real estate or business or law degrees with concentrations in real estate.

However, many teachers offering instruction at park district or adult enrichment classes are hired based more on their specific skills. For example, a person with expertise in real estate sales will be a prime candidate to conduct property sales training courses.

Certification or Licensing

The REEA offers the distinguished real estate instructor (DREI) certification to those who complete training and successfully pass an examination. This designation is awarded to individuals who have proven knowledge of their industry and excellent teaching experience in a classroom setting. The DREI certification must be renewed every three years. Contact the REEA for more information on this particular certification as well as other links to industry certification opportunities as accredited by the National Association of Realtors.

Other Requirements

As a teacher, you should be able to deal with students at different skill levels, including some who might not have learned proper study habits or who have a different first language. This requires patience, as well as the ability to track the progress of each individual student. Good communication skills are essential, as you'll need to explain things clearly and to answer questions completely.

EXPLORING

Some high schools offer real estate classes as part of their business curriculum. If this is the case at your school, enroll in such classes and take the initiative to discuss your career choice with the teacher. This is a great way to learn about the highs and lows of the industry, plus you'll get a professional's opinion on your future goals.

Registering for a continuing education or vocational education course at your local park district or community college is another way of discovering the skills and disciplines needed to succeed in this field.

Are you wondering if you have what it takes to be a teacher? Try volunteering in your school's peer tutoring program. Not only will

Career and Academic
Advising Center

you be introduced to the requirements of teaching, but also you'll more than likely earn community service points needed to graduate high school. You could also volunteer to assist in special educational activities at a nursing home, church, synagogue, mosque, or community center.

EMPLOYERS

Adult education teachers, including those teaching real estate classes, can find work in a variety of different schools and education programs. Community and junior colleges offer classes in real estate ranging from property management and appraisal to broker administration. Park districts often have adult enrichment classes available in a variety of real estate–related interests.

Teachers are also hired for long-distance education programs and to lead continuing education courses for corporations and professional associations.

STARTING OUT

Most people entering this field have some professional experience in real estate, a desire to share that knowledge with other adults, and a teaching certificate or academic degree. Real estate teachers with previous practical experience in the market are highly regarded.

When pursuing work as a real estate teacher, you should contact colleges, private trade schools, vocational high schools, or other appropriate institutions that have real estate programs in place to receive additional information about employment opportunities. You can also visit the REEA website, which posts available jobs nationwide.

Many colleges, technical schools, and state departments of education offer job lines or bulletin boards of job listings. Check with your area park district for possible employment opportunities. You can also often find job openings in the classifieds of local newspapers or journals. Try the Vandema website (http://www.vandema.com/ Journals.htm) for a list of magazines pertaining to the commercial real estate industry.

ADVANCEMENT

Advancement for a skilled educator teaching classes at a community college or park district may mean a larger class load, higher pay, or additional teaching assignments dealing with different real estate specialties. They may also work towards a goal of someday teaching full time at a larger college or university. Teaching at this level may require a master's degree or doctorate.

Many educators, especially those with a good reputation, are tapped to speak at real estate seminars or provide continuing education classes at industry conferences.

EARNINGS

Earnings vary widely according to the subject, the number of courses taught, the teacher's experience, and the geographic region where the institution is located. According to the U.S. Department of Labor, self-enrichment education teachers earned an average salary of $31,530 in 2004. The lowest paid 10 percent of these workers made less than $16,890, while the highest-paid 10 percent earned $62,100 or more.

Because many real estate teachers are employed part time, they are often paid by the hour or by the course, with no health insurance or other benefits. Hourly rates range from $6 to $50.

WORK ENVIRONMENT

Working conditions vary according to the type of class being taught, the location, and the number of students participating. Courses are usually taught in a classroom setting but may also be in a work setting, conference room, or online. Those teaching at conferences or training real estate professionals at their offices often travel to the conference or work site. Class sizes vary, ranging from one-on-one instruction to large lectures attended by many individuals.

High school and college real estate teachers only work nine or 10 months a year, with summers off. Part-time teachers work 20 hours or less, depending on how many classes they teach. Some real estate teachers, especially those employed in nonacademic settings, primarily work in the evenings or on weekends, though many corporate trainers will work during regular office hours.

OUTLOOK

Employment opportunities for real estate educators will continue to be good. Professionals are needed to teach those interested in entering the field, or give additional training to those wanting career advancement.

Teaching opportunities can be found at any college or university offering undergraduate and graduate degrees in real estate. However, the majority of employment opportunities can be found at the local level—at high schools, junior colleges, proprietary schools, or park districts. Also, many real estate corporations, financial institutions, or law firms that deal with real estate issues want their employees trained in the latest skills and technology. They often hire real estate educators to conduct at work training seminars or conferences to present the latest developments in say, real estate tax law, or licensure reviews.

It should be noted that the nation's economy could drastically alter the direction and growth of this industry. A weak economy, high unemployment, or higher interest rates could deter the public from purchasing new homes, or stymie business construction or commercial rentals—which may translate to a reduced demand for real estate educators and trainers.

FOR MORE INFORMATION

For information about conferences and publications, contact
American Association for Adult and Continuing Education
10111 Martin Luther King, Jr. Highway, Suite 200C
Bowie, MD 20720
Tel: 301-459-6261
http://www.aaace.org

For information about publications, current legislation, and programs, contact
Association for Career and Technical Education
1410 King Street
Alexandria, VA 22314
Tel: 800-826-9972
Email: acte@acteonline.org
http://www.acteonline.org

For industry news and employment opportunities, contact
National Association of Realtors
430 North Michigan Avenue
Chicago, IL 60611
Tel: 800-874-6500
Email: InfoCentral@realtor.org
http://www.realtor.org

Real Estate Lawyers

QUICK FACTS

School Subjects
English
Government
Speech

Personal Skills
Communication/ideas
Leadership/management

Work Environment
Primarily indoors
Primarily multiple locations

Minimum Education Level
Law degree

Salary Range
$48,630 to $97,420 to
$125,000

Certification or Licensing
Required by all states

Outlook
About as fast as the average

DOT
110

GOE
04.02.01

NOC
4112

O*NET-SOC
23-1011.00

OVERVIEW

Lawyers who specialize in legal issues regarding real estate are called *real estate lawyers* or *real estate attorneys.* They provide advice on title and deed transfers, mortgage contracts, financing options, and other real estate topics. Real estate lawyers handle private, industrial, and commercial holdings. The American College of Real Estate Lawyers is a nationwide organization that promotes high professional standards in the practice of real estate law.

HISTORY

The tradition of governing people by laws has been established over centuries. Societies have built up systems of law that have been studied and drawn upon by later governments. The earliest known law is the Code of Hammurabi, developed about 1800 B.C. by the ruler of the Sumerians. Another early set of laws was the law of Moses, known as the Ten Commandments. Every set of laws, no matter when they were introduced, has been accompanied by the need for someone to explain those laws and help others live under them.

The great orators of ancient Greece and Rome set up schools for young boys to learn by apprenticeship the many skills involved in pleading a law case. To be an eloquent speaker was the greatest advantage. The legal profession has matured since those earlier times; a great deal of training and an extensive knowledge of legal matters are required of the modern lawyer and judge.

Much modern European law was organized and refined by legal experts assembled by Napoleon (1769–1821); their body of law was known as the Napoleonic Code. English colonists coming to America brought English common law, from which American laws have grown. In areas of the United States that were heavily settled by Spanish colonists, there are traces of Spanish law. As the population in the country grew, along with business, those who knew the law were in high demand.

Today, many lawyers choose to specialize in a particular area of the law. Real estate law, for example, deals with legal issues regarding the sale or rental of property, as well as construction-related issues.

THE JOB

Real estate lawyers handle all legal issues involving real property transactions such as the transfer of titles and deeds, obtaining mortgages, zoning, and tenant concerns. Their knowledge in real estate law is essential whether working on the sale of a bungalow or a multimillion-dollar skyscraper development. Individuals may retain the services of a lawyer to help them negotiate complicated details of a purchase, sale, or lease of property. Corporations also use the legal expertise of real estate lawyers when acquiring land for development, rehabbing existing property, or battling to change zoning boundaries or laws.

The purchase of a house or building can be intimidating; no wonder many people often retain lawyers to successfully guide them through this process. Lawyers first discuss the details of the purchase with their client. What type of property is the individual interested in purchasing—a single-family house, a multi-unit dwelling, a commercial property, or a mixed-use property? In the example of a home sale, the real estate lawyer may ask the following questions: What are the client's present living arrangements—do they own property, or are they currently leasing or renting? Is the offer contingent on the sale of their current residence? Does the property have a lien (a legal claim against a property to seek repayment for an unpaid debt) against it? Lawyers may also be asked to give advice or referrals regarding financing options, real estate agencies, mortgage brokers, or home inspectors. Lawyers will also follow the same steps when representing the seller. In addition, they may draft a property disclosure report, which by law lists any relevant information such as past flooding, presence of mold, or other concerns. Lawyers will review any pending contracts or riders, explain confusing terminology, initiate any changes, or draft/execute a punch list—a list of issues that need to be addressed before the sale is complete—before closing time.

Lawyers also represent their clients at closing. They make sure contracts and other documents are in order, tax and escrow calculations are accurate, and answer any questions from their clients. For cases under litigation, lawyers will represent their client in court.

Owners of a multi-unit apartment building often enlist the expertise of a real estate lawyer to help with problem tenants. Condominium homeowner's associations often hire a real estate expert to draft or review their by-laws—a list of regulations to be followed by members. Lawyers may also prepare a declaration—a list of regulations, which helps form a sense of unity with homeowners within a subdivision or living community.

Real estate lawyers may also work on larger, multi-property cases. They are often retained by big corporations to negotiate the sale or purchase of a high-rise building, office building, warehouse, or open parcel of land. In such cases, titles must be inspected and zoning laws reviewed. Sometimes the lawyer finds it necessary to initiate the process of rezoning the desired location from residential to commercial, or vice versa. Lawyers may also help in bidding for the property's final price.

Local governments also retain the services of real estate lawyers to help with various projects. For example, if town officials want to build an entertainment and sports complex on an undeveloped piece of land, lawyers may need to investigate public records and deeds to establish title to the property. They then negotiate a fair price with the owner. They also handle zoning issues, land inspections, and surveyor's reports before construction can begin.

REQUIREMENTS

High School

A high school diploma, a college degree, and three years of law school are minimum requirements for a law degree. A high school diploma is a first step on the ladder of education that a lawyer must climb. If you are considering a career in law, courses such as government, history, social studies, and economics provide a solid background for entering college-level courses. Speech courses are also helpful to build strong communication skills necessary for the profession. Take as many writing classes as possible during high school to strengthen your writing skills. Lawyers spend a tremendous amount of time writing briefs, contracts, and depositions for their cases. Also take advantage of any computer-related classes or experience you can get, because lawyers often use technology to research and interpret the law, from surfing the Internet to searching legal databases.

Postsecondary Training

To enter a law school approved by the American Bar Association (ABA), you must satisfactorily complete at least three, and usually four, years of college work. Most law schools do not specify any particular courses for prelaw education. Usually a liberal arts track is most advisable, with courses in English, history, economics, social sciences, logic, and public speaking. A college student planning to specialize in real estate law might also take courses significantly related to this area, such as business or economics. Those interested should contact several law schools to learn more about any special requirements and to see if they will accept credits from the college the student is planning to attend. It would also be wise to investigate the school's real estate law program.

Most law schools require that applicants take the Law School Admission Test (LSAT), where prospective law students are tested on their critical thinking, writing, and reasoning abilities.

Currently, 191 law schools in the United States are approved by the ABA; others, many of them night schools, are approved by state authorities only. Most of the approved law schools, however, do have night sessions to accommodate part-time students. Part-time courses of study usually take four years. The ABA currently does not accredit online law education programs.

Law school training in real estate consists of required courses such as legal writing and research, commercial real estate finance, public housing redevelopment, real estate investment and transactions, and real estate structuring. A degree of juris doctor (J.D.) or bachelor of laws (LL.B.) is usually granted upon graduation.

Certification or Licensing

Every state requires that lawyers be admitted to the bar of that state before they can practice. They require that applicants graduate from an approved law school and that they pass a written examination in the state in which they intend to practice. In a few states, graduates of law schools within the state are excused from these written examinations. After lawyers have been admitted to the bar in one state, they can practice in another state without taking a written examination if the states have reciprocity agreements; however, they will be required to meet certain state standards of good character and legal experience and pay any applicable fees.

Other Requirements

Many lawyers who specialize in real estate law also carry a brokers' license. A real estate broker acts as an agent for others in buying or selling property. Licensure is obtained after sufficient coursework and the successful completion of an examination. Check with your state for specific licensure requirements as they may differ from state to state.

EXPLORING

If you think a career as a lawyer might be right for you, there are several ways you can find out more about it before making a final decision. First, sit in on a trial or two at your local or state courthouse. Try to focus mainly on the lawyer and take note of what they do. Write down questions you have and terms or actions you don't understand. Then, talk to your guidance counselor and ask for help in setting up a telephone or in-person interview with a lawyer. Ask questions and get the scoop on what those careers are really all about. Also, talk to your guidance counselor or political science teacher about starting or joining a job-shadowing program. Can they connect you with a law firm in your area that specializes in real estate law? Job shadowing programs allow you to follow a person in a certain career around for a day or two to get an idea of what goes on in a typical day. You may even be invited to help out with a few minor duties.

You can also search the World Wide Web for general information about lawyers and current court cases. After you've done some research and talked to a lawyer, and you still think you are destined for law school, try to get a part-time job in a law office. Ask your guidance counselor for help.

If you are already in law school, you might consider becoming a student member of the American Bar Association. Student members receive *Student Lawyer,* a magazine that contains useful information for aspiring lawyers. Sample articles from the magazine can be read at http://www.abanet.org/lsd/studentlawyer. Another ABA publication, the *Real Estate Quarterly Report* (http://www.abanet.org/rppt/publications/quarterlyreports/home.html), summarizes and comments on relevant cases in real estate law. It is available for a fee from the ABA.

EMPLOYERS

Private law firms specializing in real estate law are just one avenue of employment for lawyers, either as an associate, or sole practitioner.

Real estate lawyers may also hold positions as house counsel for businesses, such as a real estate brokerage firm or developer. Some may choose to represent banks and mortgage companies. Others may be employed by local government to work on zoning laws or other real estate-related legal issues.

STARTING OUT

The first steps to entering the law profession are graduation from an approved law school and passing a state bar examination. Usually beginning lawyers do not go into solo practice right away. It is often difficult to become established, and additional experience is helpful to the beginning lawyer. Also, most lawyers do not specialize in a particular branch of law without first gaining experience. Beginning lawyers usually work as assistants to experienced real estate lawyers. At first they do mainly research and routine work. After a few years of successful experience, they may be promoted to junior partner, or be ready to go out on their own and specialize in real estate law. Other choices open to the beginning lawyer include joining an established law firm or entering into partnership with another lawyer. Positions are also available with banks, business corporations such as large title and mortgage companies, insurance companies, and with government agencies at different levels.

Many new lawyers are recruited by law firms or other employers directly from law school. Recruiters come to the school and interview possible hires. Other new graduates can get job leads from local and state bar associations.

You may also want to check out the ABA website, which often posts employment opportunities and job fairs in its Career Resource section. State bar associations will also provide job leads located in their state. Use the Internet to find out if your state has an association catering to the interests of real estate lawyers.

ADVANCEMENT

Lawyers with outstanding ability can expect to go a long way in their profession. Novice lawyers generally start as law clerks, but as they prove themselves and develop their abilities, many opportunities for advancement will arise. They may be promoted to junior partner in a law firm or establish their own practice. Lawyers may enter politics and become mayors, congressmen, or other government leaders. Others may become judges specializing in real estate law. Top positions are available in business, too, for the qualified lawyer. Lawyers working for the federal government advance according to the civil service system. Experienced lawyers may also choose to teach real estate law at colleges and universities.

EARNINGS

Incomes generally increase as the lawyer gains experience and becomes better known in the field. The beginning lawyer in solo practice may barely make ends meet for the first few years. According to the National Association for Law Placement, 2005 median salaries for new lawyers ranged from $67,500 for lawyers employed by firms of two to 25 attorneys to $125,000 for lawyers employed by firms of 501 or more attorneys.

Experienced lawyers earn salaries that vary depending on the type, size, and location of their employers. According to the U.S. Department of Labor, the 2004 median salary for practicing lawyers was $97,420, although some senior partners earned well over $1 million a year. Ten percent earned less than $48,630. General attorneys in the federal government received $101,420 in 2003. State and local government attorneys generally made less, earning $70,430 and $75,760, respectively, in 2003.

WORK ENVIRONMENT

Law offices are usually pleasant, although busy, places to work. Lawyers also spend significant amounts of time in law libraries or record rooms, and in the homes and offices of clients. They may also do onsite visits or investigations of property for a particular case. They may represent clients at closings or court appearances.

Often real estate lawyers have to work long hours, spending evenings and weekends preparing cases and materials and working with clients. In addition to the work, the lawyer must always keep up with the latest developments in the industry. Also, it takes a long time to become a qualified lawyer, and it may be difficult to earn an adequate living until the lawyer gets enough experience to develop an established private practice.

Real estate lawyers who are employed at law firms must often work grueling hours to advance in the firm. Spending long weekend hours doing research and interviewing people should be expected. Some travel may be necessary, especially when dealing with property located out of state, or if the law firm has satellite offices.

OUTLOOK

According to the *Occupational Outlook Handbook*, employment for lawyers is expected to grow about as fast as the average through 2012, but record numbers of law school graduates have created strong competition for jobs, even though the number of graduates has begun to level off. Continued population growth and typical business activities will create a steady demand for lawyers who specialize in real estate law. Opportunities may be plentiful in areas of the United States experiencing high population growth, such as the Southwestern states. An increase in population can translate to private and commercial construction needs.

Law services will be more accessible to the middle-income public with the popularity of prepaid legal services and clinics. However, stiff competition has and will continue to urge some lawyers to look outside the legal profession for employment. Administrative and managerial positions in real-estate companies, banks, insurance firms, and government agencies are typical areas where legal training is useful.

The top 10 percent of the graduating seniors of the country's best law schools will have more opportunities with well-known law firms and jobs on legal staffs of corporations, in government agencies, and in law schools in the next few decades. Lawyers in solo practice will find it hard to earn a living until their practice is fully established. The best opportunities exist in small towns or suburbs of large cities, where there is less competition and new lawyers can meet potential clients more easily.

Graduates with lower class rankings and from lesser-known schools may have difficulty in obtaining the most desirable positions.

FOR MORE INFORMATION

For information about law student services, academic programs, and publications offered by the ABA, contact
American Bar Association (ABA)
321 North Clark Street
Chicago, IL 60610
Tel: 312-988-5522
Email: abasvcctr@abanet.org
http://www.abanet.org

For information about membership requirements, contact
American College of Real Estate Lawyers
One Central Plaza

11300 Rockville Pike, Suite 903
Rockville, MD 20852
Tel: 301-816-9811
http://www.acrel.org

For information on law programs, contact
Association of American Law Schools
1201 Connecticut Avenue, NW, Suite 800
Washington, DC 20036-2717
Tel: 202-296-8851
Email: aals@aals.org
http://www.aals.org

For information on choosing a law school, law careers, salaries, and alternative law careers, contact
National Association for Law Placement
1025 Connecticut Avenue, NW, Suite 1110
Washington, DC 20036-5413
Tel: 202-835-1001
Email: info@nalp.org
http://www.nalp.org

Real Estate Writers

OVERVIEW

Writers who cover the real estate industry are referred to as *real estate writers*. They report on trends in housing developments, commercial business transactions, architecture, real estate financial concerns, and other topics for inclusion in print, broadcast, or online media. The National Association of Real Estate Editors is a nationwide group dedicated to advancing the careers of editors, writers, columnists, and freelancers specializing in real estate–related news.

HISTORY

The modern publishing age began in the 18th century. Printing became mechanized, and the novel, magazine, and newspaper developed. The first newspaper in the American colonies appeared in the early 18th century, but it was Benjamin Franklin (1706–90) who, as editor and writer, made the *Pennsylvania Gazette* one of the most influential in setting a high standard for his fellow American journalists. Franklin also published the first magazine in the colonies, *The American Magazine,* in 1741.

Advances in the printing trades, photoengraving, retailing, and the availability of capital produced a boom in newspapers and magazines in the 19th century. Further mechanization in the printing field, such as the use of the Linotype machine, high-speed rotary presses, and special color reproduction processes, set the stage for still further growth in the book, newspaper, and magazine industry.

In addition to the print media, the broadcasting industry has contributed to the development of the professional writer. Radio,

QUICK FACTS

School Subjects
Business
English
Journalism

Personal Skills
Communication/ideas
Helping/teaching

Work Environment
Primarily indoors
Primarily one location

Minimum Education Level
Bachelor's degree

Salary Range
$23,700 to $45,460 to $87,660

Certification or Licensing
None available

Outlook
About as fast as the average

DOT
131

GOE
01.02.01

NOC
5121

O*NET-SOC
27-3043.00

television, and the Internet are sources of information, education, and entertainment that provide employment for thousands of journalistic writers.

Many newspapers now have special sections or columns devoted to a particular topic of interest to readers—such as real estate. Entire magazines cover different aspects of the real estate industry, from construction to real estate sales and management. Tremendous growth in the real estate industry has resulted in increased coverage and the need for talented writers to report and comment on the news. Today, real estate–related topics are covered in newspapers, popular magazines, industry journals and websites, and broadcast media.

THE JOB

Real estate writers report on developments in the real estate industry; their reports appear in a variety of media—print, broadcast, or online. They may also prepare marketing material for industry associations.

Staff writers employed by real estate–related magazines and journals write news stories or feature articles. Topics vary, but all deal with real estate issues. For example, staff writers may be assigned finance-based articles debating the merits of interest-only loans vs. traditional fixed-rate loans; articles detailing the green building movement's effect on modern architecture; or business-related articles such as the estimated economic effects of the development of a large tract of commercial property in a rundown business district. Many staff writers work on different articles as assigned by editors; some are permanently assigned a particular area of interest, or beat.

A reporter who is assigned real estate-related stories on a regular basis is called a *real estate columnist*. Columnists are regarded as experts in their field. Aside from regular written articles, columnists may answer real estate questions from readers. Their work may appear in a newspaper's daily edition or Sunday special section, or in a monthly magazine. Oftentimes, their photo accompanies their byline.

Critics are reporters with extensive knowledge of a particular field—such as real estate. For example, architectural critics may comment on the esthetic effects of a new skyscraper on a city's skyline or decry the destruction of 200-year-old row houses in a rapidly gentrifying area. Critics usually have additional training or education related to their industry. The architectural critic for the

Chicago Tribune, for example, holds degrees in architecture and environmental design.

Real estate writers work for a variety of media. They may write material for textbooks used in real estate classes. Others may work for the public relations department of an organization or association producing newsletters or press releases. They may also place reports on behalf of a news station or a real estate website.

When working with a new assignment, writers begin gathering as much information as possible about the subject through library research, interviews, the Internet, observation, and other methods. They keep extensive notes from which they will draw material for their project. Once the material has been organized and arranged in logical sequence, writers prepare a written outline. The process of developing a piece of writing is exciting, although it can also involve detailed and solitary work. After researching an idea, a writer might discover that a different perspective or related topic would be more effective, entertaining, or marketable.

When working on assignment, writers usually submit their outlines to an editor or other company representative for approval. Then they write a first draft, trying to put the material into words that will have the desired effect on their audience. They often rewrite or polish sections of the material as they proceed, always searching for just the right way of imparting information or expressing an idea or opinion. A manuscript may be reviewed, corrected, and revised numerous times before a final copy is submitted. Even after that, an editor may request additional changes.

Real estate writers can be employed either as in-house staff or as freelancers. Pay varies according to experience and the position, but freelancers must provide their own office space and equipment such as computers and fax machines. Freelancers also are responsible for keeping tax records, sending out invoices, negotiating contracts, and providing their own health insurance. Freelancers obtain assignments by sending out query letters and writing samples to publications and organizations. While there is much freedom in their daily work hours, a steady form of employment may be difficult to establish.

REQUIREMENTS

High School

While in high school, build a broad educational foundation by taking courses in English, literature, foreign languages, history, general science, business, and social studies. Such classes usually demand written reports, which will ultimately develop your writing style. It's important to also take computer classes to become familiar with computers and to improve the speed and accuracy of your keyboarding skills.

Real estate writers don't just report on property sales—they often write about the style and design of a building or community. It is a good idea to enroll in such classes as art, architecture, and design to build your knowledge of these fields.

Postsecondary Training

Most, if not all, employers seek candidates with a college education. The type of degree in demand varies from employer to employer. Many successful writers have a liberal arts background, with majors ranging from English to philosophy to social science. Still others have real estate or business degrees. Many employers desire candidates with a degree in communications or journalism. Journalism, especially, is highly regarded because of the strong emphasis on writing and industry-relevant classes such as newspaper and magazine writing, publication management, book publishing, and Internet writing.

There are some traditional colleges and universities, such as the University of Cincinnati (http://www.business.uc.edu/realestate/academics), that offer a business degree with a concentration in real estate. While this degree focuses on the business side of the industry, there are several classes that would definitely give valuable knowledge and training to any real estate editor-in-training.

In addition to formal course work, most employers look for practical writing experience. If you have worked on high school or college newspapers, yearbooks, or literary magazines, or if you have worked for small community newspapers or radio stations, even in an unpaid position, you will be a more attractive candidate. Many magazines, newspapers, and radio and television stations have summer internship programs that provide valuable training if you want to learn about the publishing and broadcasting businesses. Interns do many simple tasks, such as running errands and answering phones, but some may be asked to perform research, conduct interviews, or even write some minor pieces. Turn to the Internet for a list of publications covering the real estate industry. Many magazines post their writer's guidelines, or any job openings. Go to http://www.vandema. com for links to real estate journals and publications.

Other Requirements

To be a real estate writer, you should be creative and able to express ideas clearly, have a broad general knowledge, be skilled in research techniques, and be computer literate. Other assets include curiosity, persistence, initiative, resourcefulness, and an accurate memory. For some jobs—on a newspaper or a television newsroom, for example, where the activity is hectic and deadlines are short—the ability to concentrate and produce under pressure is essential. Above all, you should have a strong interest in real estate–related issues and topics.

EXPLORING

As a high school or college student, you can test your interest and aptitude in the field of writing by serving as a reporter or writer on school newspapers, yearbooks, and literary magazines. Various writing courses and workshops will offer you the opportunity to sharpen your writing skills.

Small community newspapers and local radio stations often welcome contributions from outside sources, although they may not have the resources to pay for them. Jobs in bookstores, magazine shops, and even newsstands will offer you a chance to become familiar with various publications.

You can also obtain information on writing as a career by visiting local newspapers, publishers, or radio and television stations and interviewing some of the writers who work there. Contact a local real estate company and find out if it has any part-time employment opportunities; this is a great way to familiarize yourself with the industry.

The National Association of Real Estate Editors (NAREE) does not offer student membership status, but it does allow public access to its archive of industry news developments and newsletters at its website. Check out these sections to get a feel for the real estate world.

Reading is a great way to explore the real estate industry. Don't limit yourself to newspapers. Browse through industry journals such as *Realtor Magazine* (http://www.realtor.org/rmodaily.nsf), a leading publication sponsored by the National Association of Realtors that covers real estate business and news.

EMPLOYERS

Real estate writers can find employment with all types of media—print, broadcast, and online. The most obvious sources of employment are with newspapers and industry journals, but don't count out industry associations, educational publications, law firms specializing in real estate law, and the government.

The major newspaper, magazine, and book publishers and broadcasting companies account for the concentration of journalistic writers in large cities such as New York, Chicago, Los Angeles, Boston, Philadelphia, San Francisco, and Washington, D.C. Opportunities with small publishers and broadcasting companies can be found throughout the country. Freelance writers can work from a home base and report on topics per assignment.

STARTING OUT

A fair amount of experience is required to gain a high-level position in the field. Most real estate writers start out in entry-level positions such as junior staff writer, or editorial assistant. Don't be discouraged if your first writing job is not related to real estate. It is more important to get solid writing experience under your belt, and then move the direction of your writing to real estate–related topics.

Entry-level jobs may be listed with college career services offices, or obtained by applying directly to the employment departments of individual publishers or broadcasting companies. Graduates who previously served internships with these companies often have the advantage of knowing someone who can give them a personal recommendation. Want ads in newspapers and trade journals are another source for jobs. Because of the competition for positions, however, few vacancies are listed with public or private employment agencies. Don't forget to check association websites, which often post job openings, dates of upcoming job fairs, and other networking opportunities. The NAREE, for example, holds an annual convention giving editors, reporters, columnists, freelancers, and authors who cover the real estate industry a chance to discuss trends and network with their peers.

Get your clippings in order, especially those that are real estate related. Employers usually are interested in samples of published writing. These are often assembled in an organized portfolio or scrapbook. Bylined or signed articles are more credible (and, as a result, more useful) than stories whose source is not identified.

Beginning positions as junior staff writers usually involve library research, preparation of rough drafts for part or all of a report, cataloging, and other related writing tasks. At times, they may be given an assignment to complete independently. Such tasks are generally carried on under the supervision of a senior writer.

ADVANCEMENT

Most real estate writers find their first jobs as editorial, production, or research assistants. Advancement may be more rapid in small media companies, where beginners learn by doing a little bit of everything and may be given writing tasks immediately. At large publishers or broadcast companies, duties are usually more compartmentalized. Assistants in entry-level positions are assigned such tasks as research and fact checking, but it generally takes much longer to advance to full-scale writing duties.

Promotion into higher-level positions may come with the assignment of more important articles and stories to write, or it may be the result of moving to another company. A staff writer at a real estate magazine that covers the Midwest may switch to a similar position at a more prestigious publication that covers the entire United States. Or a news writer may switch to a different media as a form of advancement. Newspaper writers may move to cover the industry for an online site, or broadcast real estate reports for a local television station or cable channel.

As staff writers become more experienced in a particular aspect of the real estate industry they may be permanently assigned that beat. Writers may also be given a regular by-line column. The *New York Times,* for example, has several columnists that cover the real estate industry in general, as well as special interest areas such as architecture and new housing developments. Special features usually appear in weekly sections of the paper that deal with home or housing concerns.

Freelance or self-employed writers earn advancement in the form of bigger projects and larger fees as they gain exposure and establish their reputations.

EARNINGS

In 2004, median earnings for all salaried writers were $45,460 a year, according to the U.S. Department of Labor. The lowest 10 percent earned less than $23,700, while the highest 10 percent earned $87,660 or more. Writers employed by newspaper, book, and directory publishers had annual mean earnings of $45,450; in radio and television broadcasting, $44,490; and in advertising and related services, $58,570.

In addition to their salaries, many real estate writers earn some income from freelance work. Part-time freelancers may earn from $5,000 to $15,000 a year. Freelance earnings vary widely. Full-time established freelance writers may earn $75,000 or more a year.

WORK ENVIRONMENT

Working conditions vary for journalistic writers. Although their workweek usually runs 35 to 40 hours, many writers work overtime.

A publication that is issued frequently has more deadlines closer together, creating greater pressures to meet them. The work is especially hectic on newspapers and at broadcasting companies, which operate seven days a week. Writers often work nights and weekends to meet deadlines or to cover a late-developing story.

Most writers work independently, but they often must cooperate with editors, artists, photographers, and rewriters who may have widely differing ideas of how the materials should be prepared and presented.

Physical surroundings range from comfortable private offices to noisy, crowded newsrooms filled with other workers typing and talking on the telephone. Some writers must confine their research to the library or telephone interviews, but others may travel to other cities or countries or to local sites, such as new housing developments, press conferences, groundbreaking ceremonies, or other offices.

The work is arduous, but most writers are seldom bored. Real estate writers must keep up-to-date on the latest trends and development in the industry, be it new building technology to keep heating costs low, or revisions in real estate tax laws. The most difficult element is the continual pressure of deadlines. People who are the most content as writers enjoy and work well with deadline pressure.

OUTLOOK

The employment of real estate writers is expected to increase about as fast as the average rate for all occupations through 2012, according to the U.S. Department of Labor. Employment opportunities will be available at newspapers, industry journals, book publishers, associations, and broadcast and online media. There will always be a need for real estate writers, but the current demand is greatest due to the strong construction and housing markets. This tremendous growth can be attributed to baby boomers purchasing newer, bigger primary residences and second homes, and echo boomers (baby boomers' kids) purchasing their first homes. Such activity translates to more demand for industry news coverage such as weekly columns, magazines, trade journals, and websites devoted to real estate news. Employment opportunities at associations, television, or major newspapers may be more plentiful at large metropolitan areas such as New York, Chicago, Los Angeles, or Washington, D.C. Note however, that industry growth is closely tied to the economy—future changes in mortgage rates and high unemployment can cause people to shy away from major purchases such as houses or cause a reduction in commercial construction.

People entering this field should realize that the competition for jobs is extremely keen. Beginners, especially, may have difficulty finding employment. Of the thousands who graduate each year with degrees intending to establish a career as a real estate writer, many turn to other occupations when they find that applicants far outnumber the job openings available. College students would do well to keep this in mind and prepare for an unrelated alternate career in the event they are unable to obtain a position as writer.

FOR MORE INFORMATION

For a list of accredited programs in journalism and mass communications, visit the ACEJMC website.

> **Accrediting Council on Education in Journalism and Mass Communications (ACEJMC)**
> University of Kansas School of Journalism and Mass Communications
> Stauffer-Flint Hall, 1435 Jayhawk Boulevard
> Lawrence, KS 66045-7575
> Tel: 785-864-3973
> http://www.ku.edu/~acejmc

This organization provides general educational information on all areas of journalism, including newspapers, magazines, television, and radio.

> **Association for Education in Journalism and Mass Communication**
> 234 Outlet Pointe Boulevard
> Columbia, SC 29210-5667
> Tel: 803-798-0271
> Email: aejmchq@aejmc.org
> http://www.aejmc.org

For information regarding membership, writing contests, conferences, and employment opportunities, contact

> **National Association of Real Estate Editors**
> 1003 Northwest 6th Terrace
> Boca Raton, FL 33486
> Tel: 561-391-3599
> http://www.naree.org

For industry news and employment opportunities, contact
National Association of Realtors
430 North Michigan Avenue
Chicago, IL 60611
Tel: 800-874-6500
Email: InfoCentral@realtor.org
http://www.realtor.org

The MPA is a good source of information about internships.
Magazine Publishers of America (MPA)
810 Seventh Avenue, 24th Floor
New York, NY 10019
Tel: 212-872-3700
Email: mpa@magazine.org
http://www.magazine.org

For information about working as a writer and union membership,
contact
National Writers Union
113 University Place, 6th Floor
New York, NY 10003
Tel: 212-254-0279
Email: nwu@nwu.org
http://www.nwu.org

This organization for journalists has campus and online chapters.
Society of Professional Journalists
Eugene S. Pulliam National Journalism Center
3909 North Meridian Street
Indianapolis, IN 46208
Tel: 317-927-8000
http://www.spj.org

For a list of magazines and journals specific to the commercial real
estate industry, and other related sites, visit
Vandema
http://www.vandema.com/Journals.htm

Risk Managers

OVERVIEW

Risk managers help businesses control risks and losses while maintaining the highest production levels possible. They work in industrial, service, nonprofit, and public-sector organizations. By protecting a company against loss, the risk manager helps it to improve operating efficiency and meet strategic goals.

HISTORY

Entrepreneurs have always taken steps to prevent losses or damage to their businesses. During the industrial revolution, business owners recognized that as production levels increased, risks increased at the same rate. The risks were often managed at the expense of worker health and safety.

Only since the mid-1950s, however, has risk management developed into a specialized field. With the rapid growth of technology came greater and more varied risks. Risk management changed from simply buying insurance against risks to planning a wide variety of programs to prevent, minimize, and finance losses.

THE JOB

Risk management protects people, property, and inventory. For example, factories that use hazardous chemicals require employees to wear protective clothing; department stores use closed-circuit surveillance to minimize shoplifting and vandalism; and manufacturers have a plan of action to follow should their products injure consumers. The five general categories of risks are damage to property, loss of income from property damage, injury to others, fraud or criminal acts, and death or injury of employees.

QUICK FACTS

School Subjects
Economics
Mathematics

Personal Skills
Communication/ideas
Leadership/management

Work Environment
Primarily indoors
One location with some
travel

Minimum Education Level
Bachelor's degree

Salary Range
$46,250 to $83,780 to
$115,140

Certification or Licensing
Recommended

Outlook
About as fast as the average

DOT
186

GOE
13.01.01

NOC
0111

O*NET-SOC
11-3031.00

Risk managers first identify and analyze potential losses. They examine the various risk management techniques and select the best ones, including how to pay for losses that may occur. After the chosen techniques are implemented, they closely monitor the results.

Risk management has two basic elements: risk control and risk finance. Risk control involves loss prevention techniques to reduce the frequency and lower the severity of losses. Risk managers make sure operations are safe. They see that employees are properly trained and that workers have and use safety equipment. This often involves conducting safety and loss prevention programs for employees. They make recommendations on the safe design of the workplace and make plans in case of machinery breakdowns. They examine company contracts with suppliers to ensure a steady supply of raw materials.

Risk finance programs set aside funds to pay for losses not anticipated by risk control. Some losses can be covered by the company itself; others are covered by outside sources, such as insurance firms. Risk finance programs try to reduce costs of damage or loss, and include insurance programs to pay for losses.

Large organizations often have a risk management department with several employees who each specialize in one area, such as employee-related injuries, losses to plant property, automobile losses, and insurance coverage. Small organizations have risk managers who may serve as safety and training officers in addition to handling workers' compensation and employee benefits.

REQUIREMENTS

High School

If you are interested in becoming a risk manager, you should plan on getting a bachelor's degree and may at some point consider getting an advanced degree, such as master's of business administration (MBA) or a master's in risk management. In high school, therefore, you should take classes that will prepare you for college as well as help you explore this type of work. Take plenty of mathematics classes. Also, take accounting, business, and economics if your school offers these classes. To round out your education, take a variety of science, history, government, and computer classes. And of course, take English classes, which will help you hone your research and writing skills and make you ready for college-level work.

Postsecondary Training

Risk managers generally need a college degree with a broad business background. Depending on the college or university you attend, you may be able to major in risk management or insurance. There are about 100 schools that offer courses or degrees in insurance and risk management. If your school does not offer these degrees, consider a major in other management or finance areas, such as accounting, economics, engineering, finance, law, management, or political science. No matter what your particular major, your class schedule will most likely include economics, accounting, and mathematics, such as calculus. Computer classes that deal with using a variety of software programs will also be necessary to take. Insurance and even banking classes will give you an understanding of these industries and the financial tools they use.

Certification or Licensing
Many organizations require their risk managers to earn the designation associate in risk management (ARM) or certified risk manager. The ARM program is run jointly by the American Institute for Chartered Property Casualty Underwriters and the Insurance Institute of America. You must take courses and pass exams in the following areas: risk management, risk control, and risk financing. The Institute also offers the associate in risk management for public entities certification for risk managers who are interested in working in the public sector.

The National Alliance for Insurance Education and Research offers the certified risk managers international designation. To earn this designation, you must pass exams in five courses covering all major areas of risk management.

The Risk and Insurance Management Society (RIMS) offers an advanced designation in risk management, the RIMS fellow. The program consists of workshops covering advanced issues in business, insurance, and risk management.

Other Requirements
Communications skills are important for risk managers. They must regularly interact with other departments, such as accounting, engineering, finance, human resources, environmental, legal, research and development, safety, and security. They must also be able to communicate with outside sources, such as attorneys, brokers, union officials, consultants, and insurance agents.

Risk managers must have analytical and problem-solving skills in order to foresee potential problem situations and recommend appropriate solutions. They must be able to examine and prepare reports on risk costs, loss statistics, cost-versus-benefit data, insurance costs, and depreciation of assets.

Knowledge of insurance fundamentals and risk financing is necessary. Risk managers must know loss-control issues such as employee health, worker and product safety, property safeguards, fire prevention, and environmental protection.

Management skills help risk managers set goals, plan strategies, delegate tasks, and measure and forecast results. Computer skills and familiarity with business law are also very helpful.

EXPLORING

You may wish to ask your family's insurance agent to help you contact a colleague who has commercial accounts and might introduce you to a risk manager for one of their larger clients.

The Risk and Insurance Management Society Inc. is the largest organization for risk managers. It offers books, monographs, a bimonthly newsletter, education programs, and an annual conference. Students may be able to attend local chapter meetings. The Spencer Educational Foundation, affiliated with RIMS, provides annual scholarships to academically outstanding full-time students of risk management and insurance. (See the end of this article for contact information.)

EMPLOYERS

Airlines, banks, insurance companies, manufacturers, government agencies, municipalities, hospitals, retailers, school districts, and colleges and universities employ risk managers.

STARTING OUT

College career services offices can put students in touch with recruiting officers from industries that employ risk managers. Recent graduates can also send resumes to employers of risk managers, such as corporations, service providers, government agencies, and other public and private organizations. Some risk managers join insurance companies, insurance brokerage firms, or consulting firms that provide risk management services to clients.

Some individuals gain experience and education while working in accounting or personnel departments and later move into risk management positions.

ADVANCEMENT

There is good potential for advancement in the risk management field. Many risk managers work in a related field, such as in a human resources department handling employee benefits.

Risk managers may eventually head a personnel or finance department, become a human resources director, or join the insurance industry. Some become independent consultants. Membership in professional associations that offer networking opportunities can lead to better positions in the field.

Risk managers usually hold mid-level management positions and often report to a financial officer. Some, however, become vice presidents or presidents of their organizations.

EARNINGS

Risk managers' salaries vary depending on level of responsibility and authority, type of industry, organization size, and geographic region. The U.S. Department of Labor, which classifies risk managers with financial managers, reported a median yearly income for financial managers of $83,780 in 2004. The lowest 10 percent had earnings of less than $46,250, while the top 25 percent earned more than $115,140.

Risk managers usually receive benefits, bonuses, paid vacation, health and life insurance, pensions, and stock options.

WORK ENVIRONMENT

Risk managers work in a variety of settings from schools, stores, and government agencies to manufacturers and airlines. Most work in offices, not on the production line, but they may be required to spend some time in production departments. They may have to travel to study risks in other companies or to attend seminars.

Risk managers usually work a 40-hour week, Monday through Friday. They may have to spend much of their time at a computer, analyzing statistics and preparing reports.

OUTLOOK

Since advanced technology continues to increase productivity as well as the potential for disaster, the need for risk management will continue to grow. Organizations now recognize risk management as an integral and effective tool for cost-containment. The profession will continue to gain recognition in the next decade, so salaries and career opportunities are expected to continue to escalate. The U.S. Department of Labor predicts the growth rate for financial managers (including risk managers) to be about as fast as the average for all occupations through 2012.

FOR MORE INFORMATION

For information about professional designations, contact

American Institute for Chartered Property Casualty Underwriters
Insurance Institute of America
720 Providence Road, PO Box 3016
Malvern, PA 19355-0716
Tel: 800-644-2101
Email: cserv@cpcuiia.org
http://www.aicpcu.org

For information on educational programs, research, and publications, contact

American Risk and Insurance Association
716 Providence Road, PO Box 3028
Malvern, PA 19355-3402
Tel: 610-640-1997
Email: aria@cpcuiia.org
http://www.aria.org

For information about the certified risk manager designation, contact

National Alliance for Insurance Education and Research
PO Box 27027
Austin, TX 78755-2027
Tel: 800-633-2165
Email: alliance@scic.com
http://www.scic.com

For industry news and training programs aimed at risk managers employed in municipal and state governments, contact

Public Risk Management Association
500 Montgomery Street, Suite 750
Alexandria, VA 22314
Tel: 703-528-7701
Email: info@primacentral.org
http://www.primacentral.org

For information on continuing education and the Spencer Educational Foundation, contact

Risk and Insurance Management Society Inc.
1065 Avenue of the Americas, 13th Floor
New York, NY 10018
Tel: 212-286-9292
http://www.rims.org

Surveying and Mapping Technicians

OVERVIEW

Surveying and mapping technicians help determine, describe, and record geographic areas or features. They are usually the leading assistant to the professional surveyor, civil engineer, and mapmaker. They operate modern surveying and mapping instruments and may participate in other operations. Technicians must have a basic knowledge of the current practices and legal implications of surveys to establish and record property size, shape, topography, and boundaries. They often supervise other assistants during routine surveying conducted within the bounds established by a professional surveyor. There are approximately 57,740 surveying and mapping technicians working in the United States.

HISTORY

From ancient times, people have needed to define their property boundaries. Marking established areas of individual or group ownership was a basis for the development of early civilizations. Landholding became important in ancient Egypt, and with the development of hieroglyphics, people were able to keep a record of their holdings. Eventually, nations found it necessary not only to mark property boundaries but also to record principal routes of commerce and transportation. For example, records of the Babylonians tell of their canals and irrigation ditches. The Romans surveyed and mapped their empire's principal roads. In the early days of colonial exploration, surveyors and their technical helpers were among the first and most needed workers. They established new land ownership by surveying and filing claims. Since then, precise and accurate geographical measurements have been needed to determine the location of a highway, the site of a building, the right-of-way for drainage ditches, telephone, and power lines, and for the charting of unexplored land, bodies of water, and underground mines.

Early surveying processes required at least two people. A technical scientist served as the leader, or professional surveyor. This scientist was assisted by helpers to make measurements with chains, tapes, and wheel rotations, where each rotation accounted for a known length of distance. The helpers held rods marked for location purposes and placed other markers to define important points.

As measuring instruments have become more complex, the speed, scope, and accuracy of surveying have improved. Developments in surveying and mapping technology have made great changes in the planning and construction of highway systems and structures of all kinds. For roadway route selection and design, technicians increasingly use photogrammetry, which uses plotting machines to scribe routes from aerial photographs of rural or urban areas. Route data obtained by photogrammetry may then be processed through computers to calculate land acquisition, grading, and construction costs. Photogrammetry is faster and far more accurate than former methods. In addition, new electronic distance-measuring devices have brought surveying to a higher level of precision. Technicians can measure distance more quickly, accurately, and economically than was possible with tapes, rods, and chains.

In addition to photogrammetry, the use of computers in data processing has extended surveying and mapping careers past the earth's surface. Technicians now help to make detailed maps of ocean floors and the moon. Every rocket fired from the Kennedy Space Center is tracked electronically to determine if it is on course through the use of maps made by surveyors. The technological complexity of such undertakings allows surveyors to delegate more tasks than ever to technicians.

THE JOB

As essential assistants to civil engineers, surveyors, and mapmakers, surveying and mapping technicians are usually the first to be involved in any job that requires precise plotting. This includes highways, airports, housing developments, mines, dams, bridges, and buildings of all kinds.

The surveying and mapping technician is a key worker in field parties and major surveying projects and is often assigned the position of *chief instrument worker* under the surveyor's supervision. Technicians use a variety of surveying instruments, including the theodolite, transit, level, and other electronic equipment, to measure distance or locate a position. Technicians may be *rod workers,* using level rods or range poles to make elevation and distance measurements. They may also be *chain workers,* measuring shorter distances using a surveying chain or a metal tape. During the survey, it is important to accurately record all readings and keep orderly field notes to check for accuracy.

Surveying and mapping technicians may specialize if they join a firm that focuses on one or more particular types of surveying. In a firm that specializes in land surveying, technicians are highly skilled in technical measuring and tasks related to establishing township, property, and other tract-of-land boundary lines. They help the professional surveyor with maps, notes, and title deeds. They help survey the land, check the accuracy of existing records, and prepare legal documents such as deeds and leases.

Similarly, technicians who work for highway, pipeline, railway, or power line surveying firms help to establish grades, lines, and other points of reference for construction projects. This survey information provides the exact locations for engineering design and construction work.

Technicians who work for geodetic surveyors help take measurements of large masses of land, sea, or space. These measurements must take into account the curvature of Earth and its geophysical characteristics. Their findings set major points of reference for smaller land surveys, determining national boundaries, and preparing maps.

Technicians may also specialize in hydrographic surveying, measuring harbors, rivers, and other bodies of water. These surveys are needed to design navigation systems, prepare nautical maps and charts, establish property boundaries, and plan for breakwaters, levees, dams, locks, piers, and bridges.

Mining surveying technicians are usually on the geological staffs of either mining companies or exploration companies. In recent years, costly new surveying instruments have changed the way they do their jobs. Using highly technical machinery, technicians can map underground geology, take samples, locate diamond drill holes, log drill cores, and map geological data derived from boreholes. They also map data on mine plans and diagrams and help the geologist determine ore reserves. In the search for new mines, technicians operate delicate instruments to obtain data on variations in Earth's magnetic field, its conductivity, and gravity. They use their data to map the boundaries of potential areas for further exploration.

Surveying and mapping technicians may find topographical surveys to be interesting and challenging work. These determine the contours of the land and indicate such features as mountains, lakes, rivers, forests, roads, farms, buildings, and other distinguishable landmarks. In topographical surveying, technicians help take aerial or land photographs with photogrammetric equipment installed in an airplane or groundstation that can take pictures of large areas. This method is widely used to measure farmland planted with certain crops and to verify crop average allotments under government production planning quotas.

A large number of survey technicians are employed in construction work. Technicians are needed from start to finish on any job. They check the construction of a structure for size, height, depth, level, and form specifications. They also use measurements to locate the critical construction points as specified by design plans, such as corners of buildings, foundation points, center points for columns, walls, and other features, floor or ceiling levels, and other features that require precise measurements and location.

Technological advances such as the Global Positioning System (GPS) and Geographic Information Systems (GIS) have revolutionized surveying and mapping work. Using these systems, surveying teams can track points on the Earth with radio signals transmitted from satellites and store this information in computer databases.

REQUIREMENTS

High School

If you are interested in becoming a surveying and mapping technician, take mathematics courses, such as algebra, geometry, and trigonometry, as well as mechanical drawing. Physics, chemistry, and biology are other valuable classes that will help you gain laboratory experience. Reading, writing, and comprehension skills as well as knowledge of computers are also vital in surveying and mapping, so English and computer science courses are also highly recommended.

Postsecondary Training

Though not required to enter the field, graduates of accredited postsecondary training programs for surveying, photogrammetry, and mapping are in the best position to become surveying and mapping technicians. Postsecondary training is available from institutional programs and correspondence schools. These demanding technical programs generally last two years with a possible field study in the summer. First-year courses include English, composition, drafting, applied mathematics, surveying and measurements, construction materials and methods, applied physics, statistics, and computer applications. Second-year courses cover subjects such as technical physics, advanced surveying, photogrammetry and mapping, soils and foundations, technical reporting, legal issues, and transportation and environmental engineering. Contact the American Congress on Surveying and Mapping (ACSM) for a list of accredited programs (see the end of this article for contact information).

With additional experience and study, technicians can specialize in geodesy, topography, hydrography, or photogrammetry. Many graduates of two-year programs later pursue a bachelor's degree in surveying, engineering, or geomatics.

Certification or Licensing

Unlike professional land surveyors, there are no certification or licensing requirements for becoming a surveying and mapping technician. However, technicians who seek government employment must pass a civil service examination.

Many employers prefer certified technicians for promotions into higher positions with more responsibility. ACSM offers the voluntary survey technician certification at four levels. With each level, the technician must have more experience and pass progressively challenging examinations. If the technician hopes to one day work as a surveyor, he or she must be specially certified to work in his or her state.

Other Requirements

To be a successful surveying and mapping technician, you must be patient, orderly, systematic, accurate, and objective in your work. You must be willing to work cooperatively and have the ability to think and plan ahead. Because of the increasing technical nature of their work, you must have computer skills to be able to use highly complex equipment such as GPS and GIS technology.

EXPLORING

One of the best opportunities for experience is to work part time or during your summer vacation for a construction firm or a company involved in survey work. Even if the job does not involve direct contact with survey crews, you may be able to observe their work and converse with them to discover more about their daily activities. Another possibility is to work for a government agency overseeing land use. The Bureau of Land Management, for example, has employment opportunities for students who qualify, as well as many volunteer positions. The Forest Service also offers temporary positions for students.

EMPLOYERS

There are approximately 57,740 surveying and mapping technicians working in the United States. Almost two-thirds of technicians find work with engineering or architectural service firms. The federal government also employs a number of technicians to work for the U.S. Geological Survey, the Bureau of Land Management, the National Oceanic and Atmospheric Administration, the National Geospatial-Intelligence Agency, and the Forest Service. State and local governments also hire surveying and mapping technicians to work for highway departments and urban planning agencies. Construction firms and oil, gas, and mining companies also hire technicians.

STARTING OUT

If you plan on entering surveying straight from high school, you may first work as an apprentice. Through on-the-job training and some classroom work, apprentices build up their skills and knowledge of the trade to eventually become surveying and mapping technicians.

If you plan to attend a technical institute or four-year college, contact your school's career services office for help in arranging examinations or interviews. Employers of surveying technicians often send recruiters to schools before graduation and arrange to employ promising graduates. Some community or technical colleges have work-study programs that provide cooperative part-time or summer work for pay. Employers involved with these programs often hire students full time after graduation.

Finally, many cities have employment agencies that specialize in placing technical workers in positions in surveying, mapping, construction, mining, and related fields. Check your local newspaper, telephone book, or surf the Web to see if your town offers these services.

ADVANCEMENT

Possibilities for advancement are linked to levels of formal education and experience. As technicians gain experience and technical knowledge, they can advance to positions of greater responsibility and eventually work as *chief surveyor*. To advance into this position, technicians will most likely need a two- or four-year degree in surveying and many years of experience. Also, all 50 states require surveyors to be licensed, requiring varying amounts of experience, schooling, and examinations.

Regardless of the level of advancement, all surveying and mapping technicians must continue studying to keep up with the technological developments in their field. Technological advances in computers, lasers, and microcomputers will continue to change job requirements. Studying to keep up with changes combined with progressive experience gained on the job will increase the technician's opportunity for advancement.

EARNINGS

According to the U.S. Department of Labor, the 2004 median salary for all surveying and surveying and mapping technicians, regardless of industry, was $31,020. The lowest 10 percent earned less than $19,380, and the highest 10 percent earned $51,740 or more. Technicians working for the public sector in federal, state, and local governments generally earn more per hour than those working in the private sector for engineering and architectural services. Surveying and mapping technicians working for the federal government made an average of $41,780 per year in 2004.

WORK ENVIRONMENT

Surveying and mapping technicians usually work about 40 hours a week except when overtime is necessary. The peak work period for many kinds of surveying work is during the summer months when weather conditions are most favorable. However, surveying crews are exposed to all types of weather conditions.

Some survey projects involve certain hazards depending upon the region and the climate as well as local plant and animal life. Field survey crews may encounter snakes and poison ivy. They are subject to heat exhaustion, sunburn, and frostbite. Some projects, particularly those being conducted near construction projects or busy highways, impose dangers of injury from cars and flying debris.

Unless survey technicians are employed for office assignments, their work location changes from survey to survey. Some assignments may require technicians to be away from home for varying periods of time. While on the job, technicians who supervise other workers might wear hard hats, special clothing, and protective shoes.

OUTLOOK

Surveying and mapping technicians are expected to enjoy better job prospects than other workers in the surveying field. According to the *Occupational Outlook Handbook,* employment growth is expected to be faster than the average for all occupations through 2012. This better outlook may be attributed to the lower entry requirements and lower wages than those of other technician jobs.

The need to replace workers who have either retired or transferred to other occupations will also provide opportunities. In general, technicians with more education and skill training will have more job options.

FOR MORE INFORMATION

For more information on accredited surveying programs, contact
Accreditation Board for Engineering and Technology Inc.
111 Market Place, Suite 1050
Baltimore, MD 21202-4012
Tel: 410-347-7700
http://www.abet.org

For information on careers, scholarships, certification, and educational programs, contact
American Congress on Surveying and Mapping
6 Montgomery Village Avenue, Suite 403
Gaithersburg, MD 20879
Tel: 240-632-9716
http://www.acsm.net

For information about the Bureau of Land Management and its responsibilities, visit its website.
Bureau of Land Management
Office of Public Affairs
1849 C Street, Room 406-LS
Washington, DC 20240
Tel: 202-452-5125
http://www.blm.gov

Surveyors

OVERVIEW

Surveyors mark exact measurements and locations of elevations, points, lines, and contours on or near Earth's surface. They measure distances between points to determine property boundaries and to provide data for mapmaking, construction projects, and other engineering purposes. There are approximately 124,000 surveyors, cartographers, photogrammetrists, and surveying technicians employed in the United States.

HISTORY

As the United States expanded from the Atlantic to the Pacific, people moved over the mountains and plains into the uncharted regions of the West. They found it necessary to chart their routes and to mark property lines and borderlines by surveying and filing claims.

The need for accurate geographical measurements and precise records of those measurements has increased over the years. Surveying measurements are needed for the location of a trail, highway, or road; the site of a log cabin, frame house, or skyscraper; the right-of-way for water pipes, drainage ditches, and telephone lines; and for the charting of unexplored regions, bodies of water, land, and underground mines.

As a result, the demand for professional surveyors has grown and become more complex. New computerized systems are now used to map, store, and retrieve geographical data more accurately and efficiently. This new technology has not only improved the process of surveying but extended its reach as well. Surveyors can now make detailed maps of ocean floors and the moon's surface.

THE JOB

On proposed construction projects, such as highways, airstrips, and housing developments, it is the surveyor's responsibility to make necessary measurements through an accurate and detailed survey of the area. The surveyor usually works with a field party consisting of several people. *Instrument assistants,* called *surveying and mapping technicians,* handle a variety of surveying instruments including the theodolite, transit, level, surveyor's chain, rod, and other electronic equipment. In the course of the survey, it is important that all readings be recorded accurately and field notes maintained so that the survey can be checked for accuracy.

Surveyors may specialize in one or more particular types of surveying.

Land surveyors, also called *boundary surveyors* and *cadastral surveyors,* establish township, property, and other tract-of-land boundary lines. Using maps, notes, or actual land title deeds, land surveyors survey the land, checking for the accuracy of existing records. This information is used to prepare legal documents such as deeds and leases. *Land surveying managers* coordinate the work of surveyors, their parties, and legal, engineering, architectural, and other staff involved in a project. In addition, these managers develop policy, prepare budgets, certify work upon completion, and handle numerous other administrative duties.

Highway surveyors establish grades, lines, and other points of reference for highway construction projects. This survey information is essential to the work of the numerous engineers and the construction crews who build the new highway.

Geodetic surveyors measure large masses of land, sea, and space that must take into account the curvature of Earth and its geophysical characteristics. Their work is helpful in establishing points of reference for smaller land surveys, determining national boundaries, and preparing maps. *Geodetic computers* calculate latitude, longitude, angles, areas, and other information needed for mapmaking. They work from field notes made by an engineering survey party and also use reference tables and a calculating machine or computer.

Marine surveyors measure harbors, rivers, and other bodies of water. They determine the depth of the water through measuring sound waves in relation to nearby land masses. Their work is essential for planning and constructing navigation projects, such as breakwaters, dams, piers, marinas, and bridges, and for preparing nautical charts and maps.

The ability to work with numbers and perform mathematical computations accurately and quickly is very important for surveyors. *(Jim Whitmer Photography)*

Mine surveyors make surface and underground surveys, preparing maps of mines and mining operations. Such maps are helpful in examining underground passages within the levels of a mine and assessing the volume and location of raw material available.

Geophysical prospecting surveyors locate and mark sites considered likely to contain petroleum deposits. *Oil-well directional surveyors* use sonic, electronic, and nuclear measuring instruments to gauge the presence and amount of oil- and gas-bearing reservoirs. *Pipeline surveyors* determine rights-of-way for oil construction projects, providing information essential to the preparation for and laying of the lines.

Photogrammetric engineers determine the contour of an area to show elevations and depressions and indicate such features as mountains, lakes, rivers, forests, roads, farms, buildings, and other landmarks. Aerial, land, and water photographs are taken with special equipment able to capture images of very large areas. From these pictures, accurate measurements of the terrain and surface features can be made. These surveys are helpful in construction projects and in the preparation of topographical maps. Photogrammetry is particularly helpful in charting areas that are inaccessible or difficult to travel.

Forensic surveyors have expert knowledge of surveying and many years of experience in the field. They serve as expert witnesses at trials and hearings or in lawsuits relating to industrial, automobile, maritime, or other types of accidents.

REQUIREMENTS

High School
Does this work interest you? If so, you should prepare for it by taking plenty of math and science courses in high school. Take algebra, geometry, and trigonometry to become comfortable making different calculations. Earth science, chemistry, and physics classes should also be helpful. Geography will help you learn about different locations and their characteristics. Benefits from taking mechanical drawing and other drafting classes include an increased ability to visualize abstractions, exposure to detailed work, and an understanding of perspectives. Taking computer science classes will prepare you for working with technical surveying equipment.

Postsecondary Training
Depending on state requirements, you will need some postsecondary education. The quickest route is by earning a bachelor's degree in surveying or engineering combined with on-the-job training. Other entry options include obtaining more job experience combined with a one- to three-year program in surveying and surveying technology offered by community colleges, technical institutes, and vocational schools.

Certification or Licensing
All 50 states require that surveyors making property and boundary surveys be licensed or registered. The requirements for licensure vary, but most require a degree in surveying or a related field, a certain number of years of experience, and passing of examinations in land surveying. Generally, the higher the degree obtained, the less experience required. Those with bachelor's degrees may need only two to four years of on-the-job experience, while those with a lesser degree may need up to 12 years of prior experience to obtain a license. Information on specific requirements can be obtained by contacting the licensure department of the state in which you plan to work. If you are seeking employment in the

federal government, you must take a civil service examination and meet the educational, experience, and other specified requirements for the position.

Other Requirements

The ability to work with numbers and perform mathematical computations accurately and quickly is very important. Other helpful qualities are the ability to visualize and understand objects in two and three dimensions (spatial relationships) and the ability to discriminate between and compare shapes, sizes, lines, shadings, and other forms (form perception).

Surveyors walk a great deal and carry equipment over all types of terrain so endurance and coordination are important physical assets. In addition, surveyors direct and supervise the work of their team, so you should be good at working with other people and demonstrate leadership abilities.

EXPLORING

While you are in high school, begin to familiarize yourself with terms, projects, and tools used in this profession by reading books and magazines on the topic. One magazine you can take a look at online is *Professional Surveyor Magazine* at http://www.profsurv. com. One of the best opportunities for experience is a summer job with a construction firm or company that requires survey work. Even if the job does not involve direct contact with survey crews, it will offer an opportunity to observe surveyors and talk with them about their work.

Some colleges have work-study programs that offer on-the-job experience. These opportunities, like summer or part-time jobs, provide helpful contacts in the field that may lead to future full-time employment. If your college does not offer a work-study program and you can't find a paying summer job, consider volunteering at an appropriate government agency. The U.S. Geological Survey and the Bureau of Land Management usually have volunteer opportunities in select areas.

EMPLOYERS

According to the U.S. Department of Labor, almost two-thirds of surveying workers in the United States are employed in engineering, architectural, and surveying firms. Federal, state, and local government agencies are the next largest employers of surveying workers, and the majority of the remaining surveyors work for construction firms, oil and gas extraction companies, and public utilities. Only a small number of surveyors are self-employed.

STARTING OUT

Apprentices with a high school education can enter the field as equipment operators or surveying assistants. Those who have postsecondary education can enter the field more easily, beginning as surveying and mapping technicians.

College graduates can learn about job openings through their schools' career services offices or through potential employers that may visit their campus. Many cities have employment agencies that specialize in seeking out workers for positions in surveying and related fields. Check your local newspaper or telephone book to see if such recruiting firms exist in your area.

ADVANCEMENT

With experience, workers advance through the leadership ranks within a surveying team. Workers begin as assistants and then can move into positions such as senior technician, party chief, and, finally, licensed surveyor. Because surveying work is closely related to other fields, surveyors can move into electrical, mechanical, or chemical engineering or specialize in drafting.

EARNINGS

Surveyors earned a median annual salary of $43,980 in 2004, according to the U.S. Department of Labor. The middle 50 percent earned between $32,820 and $58,320 a year. The lowest 10 percent were paid less than $25,030, and the highest 10 percent earned $73,580 or more a year. Surveyors employed by the federal government earned annual mean salaries of $65,870; in state government, $54,930; and in local government, $49,540.

Most positions with the federal, state, and local governments and with private firms provide life and medical insurance, pension, vacation, and holiday benefits.

WORK ENVIRONMENT

Surveyors work 40-hour weeks, except when overtime is necessary to meet a project deadline. The peak work period is during the summer months when weather conditions are most favorable. However, it is not uncommon for the surveyor to be exposed to adverse weather conditions.

Some survey projects may involve hazardous conditions, depending on the region and climate as well as the plant and animal life. Survey crews may encounter snakes, poison ivy, and other plant and animal life and may suffer heat exhaustion, sunburn, and frostbite while in the field. Survey projects, particularly those near construction projects or busy highways, may impose dangers of injury from heavy traffic, flying objects, and other accidental hazards. Unless the surveyor is employed only for office assignments, the work location most likely will change from survey to survey. Some assignments may require the surveyor to be away from home for periods of time.

OUTLOOK

The U.S. Department of Labor predicts the employment of surveyors to grow about as fast as the average through 2012. The outlook is best for surveyors who have college degrees and advanced field experience. Despite slower growth, the widespread use of technology, such as the Global Positioning System and Geographic Information Systems, will provide jobs to surveyors with strong technical and computer skills.

Growth in urban and suburban areas (with the need for new streets, homes, shopping centers, schools, gas and water lines) will provide employment opportunities. State and federal highway improvement programs and local urban redevelopment programs also will provide jobs for surveyors. The expansion of industrial and business firms and the relocation of some firms to large undeveloped tracts will also create job openings. However, construction projects are closely tied to the state of the economy, so employment may fluctuate from year to year.

FOR MORE INFORMATION

For information on state affiliates and colleges and universities offering land surveying programs, contact
American Congress on Surveying and Mapping
6 Montgomery Village Avenue, Suite 403
Gaithersburg, MD 20879
Tel: 240-632-9716
http://www.acsm.net

For information on recommended books, check out the following website:

American Association for Geodetic Surveying
6 Montgomery Village Avenue, Suite 403
Gaithersburg, MD 20879
Tel: 240-632-9716
http://128.242.90.7/aags/index.html

For information on certification and student competitions, visit the following website:

National Society of Professional Surveyors
6 Montgomery Village Avenue, Suite 403
Gaithersburg, MD 20879
Tel: 240-632-9716
http://128.242.90.7/nsps/index.html

For information on photogrammetry and careers in the field, contact

American Society for Photogrammetry and Remote Sensing
5410 Grosvenor Lane, Suite 210
Bethesda, MD 20814-2160
Tel: 301-493-0290
Email: asprs@asprs.org
http://www.asprs.org

For information on volunteer opportunities with the federal government, contact

Bureau of Land Management
Office of Public Affairs
1849 C Street, Room 406-LS
Washington, DC 20240
Tel: 202-452-5125
http://www.blm.gov

U.S. Geological Survey
12201 Sunrise Valley Drive
Mail Stop 205P
Reston, VA 20192
Tel: 888-275-8747
http://www.usgs.gov

For a wealth of information on careers in surveying, visit

Measuring the World Around Us: A High-Tech Career in Professional Surveying
http://www.surveyingcareer.com

Title Searchers and Examiners

OVERVIEW

Title searchers and *examiners* conduct searches of public records to determine the legal chain of ownership for a piece of real estate. Searchers compile lists of mortgages, deeds, contracts, judgments, and other items pertaining to a property title. Examiners determine a property title's legal status, abstract recorded documents (mortgages, deeds, contracts, and so forth), and sometimes prepare and issue policy guaranteeing a title's legality. There are about 55,000 title searchers and examiners working in the United States.

HISTORY

To mortgage, sell, build on, or even give away a piece of real estate, the ownership of the land must be first proven and documented. This ownership is known as a title. Establishing a clear title, however, is not an easy task. Land may change hands frequently, and questions often arise as to the use and ownership of the property.

In the United States, most major real estate dealings are publicly recorded, usually with the county recorder, clerk, or registrar. This system began in colonial Virginia and has spread throughout the rest of the country, giving the nation a unique method for keeping track of real estate transactions. In some areas of the country, a title can be traced back 200 years or more.

Over that length of time, a parcel of land may change ownership many times. Owners divide large pieces of land into smaller parcels and may sell or lease certain rights, such as the right to mine beneath a property or run roads and irrigation ditches over it, separately from the land itself. Official records of ownership and interests in land might be contradictory or incomplete. Because of the profitability of the real estate business, the industry has devised methods of leasing and selling property, which makes the task of identifying interests in real property even more complicated and important.

THE JOB

Clients hire title searchers and examiners to determine the legal ownership of all parts and privileges of a piece of property. The client may need this information for many reasons: In addition to land sales and purchases, a lawyer may need a title search to fulfill the terms of someone's will; a bank may need it to repossess property used as collateral on a loan; a company may need it when acquiring or merging with another company; or an accountant may need it when preparing tax returns.

The work of the title searcher is the first step in the process. After receiving a request for a title search, the title searcher determines the type of title evidence to gather, its purpose, the people involved, and a legal description of the property. The searcher then compares this description with the legal description contained in public records to verify such facts as the deed of ownership, tax codes, tax parcel number, and description of property boundaries.

This task can take title searchers to a variety of places, including the offices of the county tax assessor, the recorder or registrar of deeds, the clerk of the city or state court, and other city, county, and state officials. Title searchers consult legal records, surveyors' maps, and tax rolls. Companies who employ title searchers also may keep records called indexes. These indexes are kept up-to-date to allow fast, accurate searching of titles and contain important information on mortgages, deeds, contracts, and judgments. For example, a law firm specializing in real estate and contract law probably would keep extensive indexes, using information gathered both in its own work and from outside sources.

While reviewing legal documents, the title searcher records important information on a standardized worksheet. This information can include judgments, deeds, mortgages (loans made using the property as collateral), liens (charges against the property for the satisfaction of a debt), taxes, special assessments for streets and sewers, and easements. The searcher must record carefully the sources of this information, the location of these records, the date on which any action took place, and the names and addresses of the people involved.

Using the data gathered by the title searcher, the title examiner then determines the status of the property title. Title examiners study all the relevant documents on a property, including records of marriages, births, divorces, adoptions, and other important legal proceedings, to determine the history of ownership. To verify certain facts, they may need to interview judges, clerks, lawyers, bankers, real estate brokers, and other professionals. They may summarize the legal documents they have found and use these abstracts as references in later work.

Title examiners use this information to prepare reports that describe the full extent of a person's title to a property; that person's right to sell, buy, use, or improve it; any restrictions that may exist; and actions required to clear the title. If employed in the office of a title insurance company, the title examiner provides information for the issuance of a policy that insures the title, subject to applicable exclusions and exceptions. The insured party then can proceed to use the property, having protection against any problems that might arise.

In larger offices, a *title supervisor* may direct and coordinate the activities of other searchers and examiners.

REQUIREMENTS

High School
You must have at least a high school diploma to begin a career as a title searcher. Helpful classes include business, business law, English, social studies, computers, and typing. In addition, skills in reading, writing, and research methods are essential.

Postsecondary Training
Title searchers typically train for the field via on the job training. Because their work is more complex, title examiners usually must have completed some college course work, but a college degree is generally not a requirement. Pertinent courses for title searchers and examiners include business administration, office management, real estate law, and other types of law. In some locales, attorneys typically perform title examinations.

Certification or Licensing
A few states require title searchers and examiners to be licensed or certified. Title firms may belong to the American Land Title Association as well as to regional or state title associations. These

groups maintain codes of ethics and standards of practice among their members and conduct educational programs. Title searchers and examiners who work for a state, county, or municipal government may belong to a union representing government workers.

Other Requirements

You must be methodical, analytical, and detail-oriented in your work. As you study the many hundreds of documents that may contain important data, you need to be thorough. Overlooking important points can damage the accuracy of the final report and may result in financial loss to the client or employer. It is important not to lose sight of the reason for the title search, in addition to remembering the intricacies of real estate law.

In addition to detailed work, you may have to deal with clients, lawyers, judges, real estate brokers, and other people. This task requires good communication skills, poise, patience, and courtesy.

EXPLORING

There may be opportunities for temporary employment during the summer and school holidays at title companies, financial institutions, or law firms. Such employment may involve making copies or sorting and delivering mail, but it offers an excellent chance to see the work of a title searcher or examiner firsthand. Some law firms, real estate brokerages, and title companies provide internships for students who are interested in work as a title searcher or examiner. Information on the availability of such internships is usually available from regional or local land title associations or school guidance counselors.

EMPLOYERS

The approximately 55,000 title searchers and examiners employed in the United States work in a variety of settings. Some work for law firms, title insurance companies, financial institutions, or companies that write title abstracts. Others work for various branches of government at the city, county, or state level. Title insurance companies, while frequently headquartered in large cities, may have branches throughout the United States.

STARTING OUT

If you are interested in a career as a title searcher or examiner, you can send resumes and letters of application to firms in your area that employ these types of workers. Other leads for employment oppor-tunities are local real estate agents or brokers, government employ-ment offices, and local or state land title associations. Graduates from two- and four-year colleges usually have the added advantage of being able to consult their college career services offices for addi-tional information on job openings.

ADVANCEMENT

Title searchers and examiners learn most of their skills on the job. They may gain a basic understanding of the title search process in a few months, using public records and indexes maintained by their employers. Over time, employees must gain a broader understand-ing of the intricacies of land title evidence and record-keeping sys-tems. This knowledge and several years of experience are the keys to advancement.

With experience, title searchers can move up to become tax exam-iners, special assessment searchers, or abstracters. With enough experience, a searcher or examiner may be promoted to title super-visor or head clerk. Other paths for ambitious title searchers and examiners include other types of paralegal work or, with further study, a law degree.

EARNINGS

According to the U.S. Department of Labor, median annual earn-ings for title examiners, abstractors, and searchers were $34,780 in 2004. Salaries ranged from less than $20,960 to more than $62,550. Title searchers and examiners may receive such fringe benefits as vacations, hospital and life insurance, profit sharing, and pensions, depending on their employers.

WORK ENVIRONMENT

Title searchers and examiners generally work a 40-hour week. Because most public records offices are open only during regular business hours, title searchers and examiners usually will not put in much overtime work, except when using private indexes and prepar-ing abstracts.

The offices in which title searchers and examiners work can be very different in terms of comfort, space, and equipment. Searchers and examiners spend much of their day poring over the fine print of legal documents and records, so they may be afflicted occasionally with eyestrain and back fatigue. Generally, however, offices are pleasant, and the work is not physically strenuous.

Because the work is conducted in a business environment, title searchers and examiners usually must dress in a businesslike manner. Dress codes, however, have become more casual recently and vary from office to office.

OUTLOOK

The health of the title insurance business is directly tied to the strength of the real estate market. In prosperous times, more people buy and sell real estate, resulting in a greater need for title searches. While the real estate business in America continues to operate during periods of recession, activity does slow a little. In general, title searchers and examiners can find consistent work in any area of the country with an active real estate market. According to the *Occupational Outlook Handbook,* employment of title searchers and examiners is expected to decline through 2012.

FOR MORE INFORMATION

For information on the title insurance industry, contact
American Land Title Association
1828 L Street, NW, Suite 705
Washington, DC 20036-5104
Tel: 800-787-2582
http://www.alta.org

Index

Entries and page numbers in **bold** indicate major treatment of a topic.